From Victim

To Victory

My story

Ramie Stenzel

with Andrew DeWitt

Cover design by Ryan Winkelman.

ISBN   978-1-7326494-4-6

You can contact Ramie Stenzel at: radicalramz@hotmail.com

Dedication

To my boys…

Micah, Rodney, and Tyler

This is my legacy.
Learn from your past and grow strong in your future.
My love for you is unconditional!

"Start children off on the way they should go
and even when they are old they will not turn from it."
Proverbs 22:6

Acknowledgements

This book has been a labor of love. I owe everything to Jesus Christ, the great forgiver. Without Jesus, the little girl who was abused and traumatized, would not have forgiveness and would not have been able to forgive those who traumatized her. I would have stayed a victim. I would still be there today. But, through the loving grace of Jesus Christ, I am victorious.

In addition, I want to thank the many men and women who have helped me along on this journey. First and foremost, I want to thank my wonderful husband, Chris. He's the love of my life, my constant companion, my encourager, comedian, and friend. I couldn't have walked through the process of forgiveness without you.

Momma Cheryl ... Thank you for taking me in and lovingly caring for me as your own. You were my advocate and momma when I needed one. I will always be your baby girl!

Margaret ... My "piano lady." Thank you for all your years of friendship, your unconditional love and wearing your knees out on my behalf. You are my angel!

Kelly ... Thank you for taking on the challenge of being my "Spiritual Momma." You have taught me to see my value and my worth, not only to God but to others. God handpicked you and I to "Do Life Together." He knew you could handle me!

Jan ... We loved hard, played hard, fought hard, and we worked even harder. I know you are cheering me on from heaven. Save me the mansion next to yours.

Sarah ... Thank you for following me in this journey! Your door was always open, your shoulder was always available to cry on, and your encouraging words were there any time I needed them. Thank you for praying for me, pushing me when I needed to be pushed and teaching me when I needed to be taught. Thank you for believing in me and encouraging me to write the book I said I would never write!

Ryan … Thanks for your artistic interpretation of my life on the cover.

There are so many others to thank. At the risk of leaving someone out (for which I apologize) I want to thank Elise, Lisa, Kelli, Karla, Beth, Teresa, Wendy, Pastor Randy, Becky, the Callahans, and Mrs. Freitag.

Preface

Twenty-seven years ago I was sitting in the social services work office in Lincoln, Nebraska with my own case file on my lap. As I opened the file, I read accounts about a little girl who had been born to a drug-addicted prostitute, who had been through the foster care system. I turned the pages and recalled the abuse and countless traumas that I endured over and over again. Eventually, I closed the file and cried. I did not want to be that little girl. The only way to escape my pain at the time was to end my own life.

Now, as I sit down to write my autobiography, I share my story through tears. My journey has been long and more than a little bumpy. Not just my mother, but my dad put me through unspeakable trauma as well.

I'm pleased to announce that because of Jesus Christ, I am not that little girl that I read about in my file. I've been made new!

Through the life giving grace of Jesus Christ, I've been able to forgive both my mother and father for all that they put me through. Jesus has given me strength I never knew possible.

I'm happy to be alive and thankful for what God has done in my life. I never thought I would have such joy, but here I am thankful and full of joy as I tell my story. My prayer is that God will show you the vast depth of his love as you read my story.

Ramie Stenzel

Forward

In the summer of 1991, I noticed Ramie as soon as I walked into the room at a Christian youth service at Grace Community Church in Denver, Colorado. I couldn't keep my eyes off her. I was just a kid going to church and wasn't going to the service looking for love, but that's exactly what I found. Without knowing her name, or anything about her, I knew we were meant to be together. It was truly love at first sight.

Early in our growing relationship she shared about her childhood and I began to understand there were bits and pieces of her broken environment and life. The more I heard, the more I was overwhelmed by her story. Since I was unable to restore what was broken in the past, I was determined to build a stable life of our own.

We got married in 1993 and have been together ever since. Our three great kids keep us hopping. From the outside you'd think we were a typical Christian church going family. But when you look behind the scenes, there is so much more. Over our years together, I have watched, witnessed, and lived with her amazing story, and the ramifications it has had in her life. Now, that she has put her story on paper in vivid detail, I've learned more with each word, sentence, and chapter. I was there with her while she recalled the details through tears and put the story into a form that others will be able to read, understand and learn from. There is so much in these pages, lessons of trials, love, forgiveness, and joy.

Somehow, through her childhood and teen years, Ramie survived. God's protection hovered over her and kept her safe in spite of terrible things she endured. A house without a foundation will fall and a ship without a keel will not survive the storms of life. In those trials, these walks through the fire, God formed her foundation, and built her like a ship with a strong keel in order to survive. Tempered steel is made when steel is put in a furnace and heated until it is red hot, then immediately immersed in oil. That's what Ramie has been through, and she's come out as tough as nails.

God entrusted me to care for Ramie. As her husband, I'm the leader of our family and her protector. Yet she has cared for me over the years.

This amazing person has so much to offer. A solid vessel that pours out to others more than her capacity should allow.

God, thank you for my anchor. Thank you for creating her form to grow old with. I pray that you bless her more as this journey continues.

Chris Stenzel

Chapter 1

Before I formed you in the womb, I knew you,
before you were born I set you apart;
I appointed you as a prophet to the nations.

Jeremiah 1:5

The white 1967 Pontiac Catalina sat in the garage as the rain poured down outside onto the shingles and dripped down to the ground. That car was my father's pride and joy. He could drone on talking about the 427 engine and everything that made the American muscle car great. He loved that car. One of my very first memories took place in that car. It was not a good memory. In fact many of my memories for my whole life fall into the category of painful or traumatic. But I remember the car, even the Royal Blue top and white wall tires. Eventually, I learned how to drive in that car, but I'm getting ahead of myself.

I remember waking up in the trunk of the car when I was only three years old. I wiggled back and forth on the hard surface in the dark and cried. On my left lay my ten-year-old sister Lisa, on my right, my eight-year-old brother David – both from my mother's first marriage. My mother had given the three of us sleeping pills and locked us in the trunk of the car. We had no blankets, no food, and no water. There was no way to measure the time. It seemed endless.

When I woke up, the darkness and cold added to my confusion. I kicked and screamed with all my might. I wiggled and squirmed bumping into my siblings. They shushed me and did their best to calm me down until the fog of confusion passed in the process of awaking from a drugged state. Together, we suffered in the confinement of a dark prison cell.

After a while, I heard the sound of the key being inserted and then there was a click as the lid of the trunk of our Pontiac opened. Lisa and David climbed out and I laid there like a panicked puppy in my sobbing mess. Through my tears I looked up at the eyes of my mother, Jane. Her brown hair flowed across her face in the breeze. Her green eyes met with mine as she bent over to pick me up. I didn't have the words to ask why she had left us alone in such a strange unsettling place, so I simply cried. Expressionless, she stood upright, settled me onto her hip and reached up to close the trunk. No sorrow. No regret. No empathy or sadness. She turned her head and walked to the kitchen as she closed the trunk behind us.

The rain had stopped and the sun had gone down. I wish I'd had the capacity to form my argument. I would have protested her actions and asked her, "Why did you do that? Where did you go?"

She brought me into the house and we sat on the recliner together. She hummed the tune to "You and Me Against the World" by Helen Reddy. I knew the song well, she always hummed it when she had done something wrong. In her distorted way, it almost seemed like an apology. I naturally conformed to her body. With my head on her chest I listened to the humming resonate.

My mother was slender in her younger years. Standing at 5' 6" she was average in many ways and would easily fit into a crowd without being noticed. I don't remember her being exceptionally beautiful, or plain, she was just my Mom. Her full name was Florene Jane Hensley, but she went by Jane. She was born July 7, 1943, the second daughter of Lawrence and Marie Hensley. The oddly named sisters Florene and Laurene were raised with the stern discipline known to military families. Her father served as a infantryman in World War II and suffered a traumatic injury. He was surgically treated for a skull fracture and returned home with a metal plate in his head. Emotionally, he was a very different man. He was violent and angry and Jane was often the recipient of his outbursts. By the time she was seventeen, she had endured too much of his abuse. She dropped out of school and ran away from home. When she didn't come home, she was disavowed and declared to be the black sheep of the family.

In an effort to deal with the pain of the memories of her father, she made an appointment with a psychiatrist. After an hour, he saw that her pain and suffering was significant and dutifully prescribed her an antidepressant medication. She took them daily and noticed a modest improvement. She continued to see him, and while he didn't provide any respite from the pain of her past, at least every time she saw him, she was able to walk away with a bottle of pills.

At the age of eighteen, she met a boy named Richard Maggard. They shared some laughs together and truly bonded when they realized that they both came from similar families. Richard suffered from a deep sadness and was comforted by a mirror image of his sadness in Jane. They thought they belonged together, but in retrospect, it's possible that they both brought each other further along the path into great sadness. It didn't take long before Jane was pregnant with their first child, Lisa and they married. A couple of years later, David came along. Married life was full of challenges, Richard struggled deeply and neither of them had any family support.

One Saturday, Jane went to work at the local diner while Richard was home with the kids. He was supposed to feed and care for them like a dutiful father. However, when Jane came home, she found a wreck of a house. The kids were locked in the basement, and Richard was nowhere to be seen. Doing her best to cope, she took an extra pill as she changed the full diapers and fed the kids their first meal of the day as the sun was setting. The following day, the episode repeated itself. The children had been left to fend for themselves all day and she had no idea where he was. In desperation, she repeated the extra pill. The following day, two pills were the norm, and soon two weren't enough and she needed more and more as the complexity of problems grew. After seven years of marriage, they had a routine. The sadness had over taken Richard, and children had become secondary to the pills.

One Sunday afternoon, Jane and her two kids found him dead in the living room, by his own hand. Jane was devastated. She called the police and as they came, she melted into the couch. Her children were forever scarred from the experience. I don't know where she went that evening or what happened to the kids, but Jane knew she needed something stronger than her pills. She found a friend who offered her something that she hoped would be helpful. For the first time, Jane took LSD.

The drug took her on a trip into a hallucinogenic euphoria. She got what she wanted, escape from reality. But along with the high came severe damage to her neurologic processing. Her memories of that night are gone forever, but they started Jane on a path from which she would never recover. Her brain began to change.

She continued to receive her professional psychiatric help. Monthly she met with the psychiatrist, and she continued the antidepressant medication. Eventually, she needed more help. They diagnosed her with bipolar disorder and schizophrenia. It's hard to say if the drugs that she was prescribed helped with her disorders or if their inappropriate use accelerated the progression. She endured electro-shock therapy and all the medication available at the time. She did get better for a time and was able to hold down a job. But relapse is the name of the game for addiction.

In 1968, while working as a waitress at a local diner, Jane met Kenny Jan Smith. He ate dinner by himself and smoked his pipe at the table. They made some small talk and hit it off. Over the next few weeks he came to see her frequently and sat at the same table each time so he could see her. He was just a few inches taller than she was and had a slight build and fading hairline. He was quick with words and dazzled her with stories. Had he been a kid living in 2019, his energetic nature would probably have been diagnosed with Attention Deficit Hyperactivity Disorder (ADHD). He compensated for it by being incredibly busy and by smoking a pipe. With something in his hands to occupy his attention, he fiddled with it constantly. Adding his favorite Nighthawk flavor tobacco, he packed it down, lit and relit the small charred bowl. He was in constant motion. He had seven pipes that he cycled through – one

for each day of the week.

He worked as a salesman for 3M National Outdoor Advertising. While she wasn't impressed with his title, he was quick witted and fun to be around. Kenny was a salesman simply through his personality. Jane was genuinely attracted to him. They shared life experiences and she quickly learned that he was divorced. His work took him far and wide, and he used his gift of gab to convince anybody he ran into to buy anything he laid in front of them. As he used every one of his tactics and techniques on Jane, the sparks started to fly. She shared the story of her husband's suicide and the two of them had plenty in common. In time, he discovered her problems with prescription medication as well as LSD. He promised to help with Jane's addictions.

Soon they were married. He bought her a glorious Wentworth townhouse with three bedrooms and a bathroom upstairs. They shopped for clothes and he bought her all the latest fashion of the late 1960s. He didn't mind spending money on himself either; he sought out surgical correction for his hairline and had hair plugs performed. And of course, his new bride needed to have a Pontiac Catalina.

He also spent a fortune on medical care. When a psychiatrist was only giving advice or medications that had previously failed, he made an appointment with another doctor. Then another. Then another. Jane knew how to quiet the demons of pain. She had been through counseling, she had repeated back to the doctors the steps she needed to take in order to get better, but she was not willing to give up the security of the drugs she had held on to for so long. When she looked at the process of dealing with the pain her father had caused her, it was easier to mask her pain rather than to deal with it.

In February 1970, though she was still taking every drug that fueled her addiction, Jane convinced Kenny that a baby would make her better. He complied and in November 13, 1970, Jane gave birth to a baby girl. I was 7 pounds, 6 ounces and had all my fingers and toes and huge blue eyes. My parents named me Sara Jan.

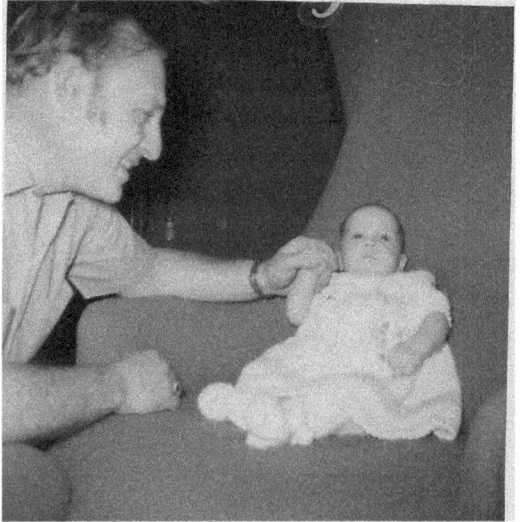

I have very few pictures of my early childhood. The few images I have depict a happy family. Though those are the traditional type of photos taken, they are far from the truth of the story.

My father traveled continually for his employment. He left our house in Omaha on Monday morning and traveled to various appointments scheduled with businesses across the country. He met with one after another selling billboard space. An excellent salesman, he brought home a substantial income. But to his family, he was merely a weekend visitor. He continued to put distance between himself and his family. This became his routine.

My mother had her own routine. By the time I was two or three years old, my mother's addiction had grown to the point where she was completely controlled and owned by the prescription medications and LSD. Not only was her physical body devastated, but also the cost for her daily use was overwhelming. The daily purchases outpaced the income she got as a waitress and even the healthy raises that Kenny got at his job. She needed an alternate source of income to enable her habit. In her desperation, she sold the only well-paying service that she had. With her husband traveling far and wide, rarely home during the week, she had men over to the house. When she placed me in the trunk of the car, she was off in the bedroom with a man who paid in cash.

The men made her feel special. Somehow the bond that they formed, though false and purely physical, made her feel loved. Of course, this lasted only momentarily. The money she made fueled her habit and she pursued her next high.

Meanwhile, I had my own routine. Sometimes it would be the trunk of the car, other times, I'd make my home in a laundry basket when she stowed me in a closet like unwanted human cargo. There were times when we were left alone. The basement was one of her favorite places to put us. She would lock the door and do whatever she did upstairs for hours, or even days. I banged on the door to get out, but she drowned out our noise with classical music. I sat in the basement, crying for hours on end, cold and hungry. This is how I learned Bach, Beethoven, and Mozart. I also remember listening to the tune "Music Box Dancer" in my personal nook.

My mother would venture into another world created by the drugs. Nobody knows what was going on in her mind as her hallucinations took over. She silently led us out of the house, down the street and into various parts of town. We had no food, shoes, or diapers. Several times, the local police officers picked the four of us up wandering the streets.

When my father came home, he would find hungry kids with full soiled diapers or none at all. Once, he tracked Jane down at the Omaha airport with all three of us. Other times, he found her at a local hotel. When he spoke to the clerk at the front desk he learned that she had checked in and stayed there for several days, while we were left alone at home.

Born to a drug addict mother, I was never a comfortable happy child. If I had been taken to a clinic familiar with children in my situation, they would have seen emotional and behavioral issues, a decreased attention span, and plenty of anxiety. They would have done a nutritional analysis and noted that I was eating whatever I could find and suffered from malnutrition. If they were to advise my drug-addicted mother about my chances of having a productive life, they would have a long list of things to change.

But she was still my mother and I still loved her.

I remember sitting on her lap with my head on her chest. She had grown over the years and was no longer a slight young woman. I snuggled down between her fat rolls in a brown recliner holding my blanket. I sucked my two fingers and was comforted by her humming and the sound of her heartbeat. She hummed the melodies to the Mozart and Bach that she loved to listen to. I enjoyed the humming. The smell of her cigarette smoke and morning after breath made me want to pull away but it was her smell and it was all I knew.

On Friday evenings, my father would return home. Exhausted after a long week of work, he wanted to head to the living room, turn on the television, sink into the couch, light his pipe, and watch a ball game. Instead, he came home to chaos. On the occasions that my mother was home, she didn't exactly run to the front door and greet him like a patient happy wife. He was usually greeted with a list of complaints. They didn't seem to care about social norms or waking the neighbors. Their fighting had no boundaries – verbal, emotional, or physical.

One night while they were yelling at one another, my sister Lisa opened a can of creamed corn and gave it to me. We watched from upstairs as they fought. Various books and décor flew across the room as they screamed at one another. The coffee table had a large centerpiece with hand blown glass grapes on grey driftwood. Jane used it like a baseball bat and struck him in the head with it. Blood ran down from his scalp. He stopped fighting long enough to examine the injury in the mirror and tended to his precious scalp. Then when he looked back at her, it was clear that he was more upset about the damage to his hair plugs than the fact that his marriage and family were crumbling all around him.

One night, a neighbor called the Omaha police department when the fighting reached a fever pitch well after midnight. Two officers visited the house and spoke with Kenny and Jane. They called it a domestic disturbance. Neither of them were hauled off to jail or received any punishment. Over time, the officers got to know both Mom and Dad on a first name basis. They would come whenever the neighbors complained, but nothing changed. Eventually my parent's marriage couldn't hold up under the weight of the household trauma.

When they divorced, my father was utterly sick and tired of my mother and everything associated with her. He made it clear that he wanted nothing to do with us children either – he signed off on all of his parental rights. I didn't know what that meant at the time, but without a second thought he cowardly signed the paper that allowed him to legally abandon us.

With my father out of the picture, my mom tumbled into a downward spiral of self-destructive behavior that culminated with a suicide attempt. She was admitted to a mental facility in Omaha for long term psychiatric care. My mother's problems were numerous. She was an addict, but she was also depressed and suicidal. Over the years, the drugs had pounded on her brain like a jackhammer.

The night she was admitted a police officer picked me up and carried me to his patrol car. I was amazed at how tall he was, and wondered where we were going. They took me to the social services office. I met a blonde lady named Elise, she wore dress pants and a polyester plaid blazer and carried a briefcase. She was a social worker who became my caseworker. I curled up in an office chair with my blanket and sucked on my fingers. All I had was my blanket and the clothes I was wearing. I waited while she made several phone calls. I was introduced to a new word, foster home. She explained that a new family would take care me. Eventually, I learned that the situation conferred upon me the title of foster child.

I was placed in a home, but don't have much memory of it. Actually over the next four years I was in three homes. I was flooded with thoughts and questions.

Why didn't they want me?

What was wrong with me?

I went from one home to another. Elise took me to her car and drove across town to Greene Avenue where she stopped in front of a tri-level green home. She knocked on the door and a short chubby lady with long brown hair opened it and smiled. It was clear that the two women knew each other.

Then lady squatted down at my level. She held out her hands with her palms up and said, "Hi baby girl, I'm Cheryl, are you hungry?"

I nodded.

She took me to her kitchen and asked me if there was anything I wanted. I saw a can of cream corn and pointed at it.

She smiled, "I can make something from that." She opened the can and set it on the counter while she got out a small pot and placed it on the stovetop (it was well before the days of the microwave oven). As she opened the refrigerator, she looked back at me. I had both hands around the can and held it against my belly as if it was my only prized possession. I dared someone to try and take it.

"Is that what you want?" she asked.

I nodded.

She gave me a spoon and I devoured it like it was the last meal on the planet. While I ate, Cheryl introduced me to her husband Roger. He assured me that their house was a safe place. Together they explained that I would be staying with them for a while.

After I had eaten, I met the other members of the family. I would be sharing a room with Tracy, who was about my age and Craig was younger. The introductions were seamless, they were used to having new people in the house. Roger was a police officer and Cheryl was a stay at home mom. I remember her hugging me all the time, treating me as one of her own.

The next morning, Cheryl woke me up early. I got dressed and ate breakfast with the rest of the family. They enrolled me in St. Mary's Catholic School. I settled into a wonderful Mid-western routine and enjoyed school. At the house there were other foster kids, most were short term, staying for a few weeks or a month or two. There were people coming and going at all hours of the day and night. The front door was like a turnstile with continuous activity in the living room, front porch, and in the yard. But I stayed there four years.

On Friday nights if we had been good we settled into the couch together and as a family we popped popcorn and watched Wonder Woman and Six Million Dollar Man on television.

At school I learned the basics of education along with a mild dose of God. My teacher, Sister Mary was a classic old nun. She dressed in a habit, and rapped my knuckles when she was inclined to do so. We probably prayed at some time during the day, usually when an ambulance went by, but really I looked forward to coloring during breaks between classes. They would hang my pictures on the walls and I got in trouble for writing my name too sloppily.

I learned a few things about the Bible, and I even saw a few at the school, but we never cracked it open to see what might be inside.

Cheryl made a big deal for every birthday. I received gifts and had a cake made for me, just like the rest of the kids. We even celebrated Christmas with the full entourage of Santa Clause, reindeer, and presents. I loved Barbie dolls and was very much a girly girl. Cheryl crocheted Tracy and I dolls that had their own babies. She fabricated them with Velcro on their hands so the baby stuck to the momma doll. She made Tracy and I each dolls of different colors so we wouldn't fight over them.

Elise came by the house and spent a little time talking with Cheryl, then came and visited with me. "How's my little princess today?"

"I'm great. Do you want to see the picture I drew at school today?"

Elise smiled, "Absolutely." She showed genuine appreciation of my art. Then she said, "We've got a special day today. We're going to see your Mom!"

I was overjoyed. "Yippee!"

We climbed into her car and headed off to her office. We waited in a little room with three chairs and a metal table.

I asked, "Where's my Mommy?"

Elise said, "She's on her way."

She told me stories and read a book to me. She checked her watch several times. Eventually, she got up and made a phone call. When she put down the phone she looked at me and quietly said, "She's not coming today."

I was devastated. I cried all the way back to Cheryl's house. She held me and let me cry, I don't remember how long I stayed in her arms.

The following week, Elise once again showed up and enjoyed my artwork. She said, "Let's go see you mother."

I was overjoyed. I remember humming Mozart all the way to the office. We waited and read books once again. And once again she did not come. My mother didn't want to see me.

I was overwhelmed with questions:

Why was I taken from my mother?

Didn't she want me?

What did I do wrong?

Over the course of a couple of years, the pattern of her missing the appointments confirmed the feeling that she had utterly and completely rejected me. I reciprocated. I emotionally detached myself from that woman. When Elise picked me up the only thing that could make me get into the car with her was the positive experience of reading books with Elise. I didn't want to see that distant stranger who was called by the name Mom. Occasionally she did show up to a meeting, and it was uncomfortable. I pushed away. I didn't want to see her. Cheryl was my mother now, she had lost her right to call me hers and I would certainly never go live with her. The only thing she taught me was how to hum. I figured that I could learn that life skill on my own. The pain of the missed visits far outweighed the benefit of the occasional time we spent together. After a while Elise stopped the meetings altogether.

I never asked questions. She never gave any answers.

During the 1978 Christmas season, my father made an appearance at Cheryl's house to meet with me. He brought me a present and had me open it right there with him. Inside the box sat a green robot piggy bank and a pink coat with fur around the collar. I had no interest in either of these things.

He could have given me just about anything that little girls play with and I would have loved it. I enjoyed Barbie dolls, hula-hoops, jump ropes, jacks, tea parties, stuffed animals, EZ bake oven, and on and on. But he gave me a robot piggy bank! Seriously? I didn't care about money at all. Why would I want a piggy bank, especially a robot one? Did he think I was a boy? Did he think I loved money? Did he not think to call Cheryl and ask what I would like? He bought me what he were interested in – money and stupid fur coats.

I thanked him for the gift and put the coat on. The coat didn't fit well and the fur was itchy on my neck.

I smiled up at him and was as polite as I could be.

My eight-year-old mind began asking questions. *After being at Cheryl's for four years, why did he show up now? What was he doing?*

Chapter 2

By the time I was eight years old, I had mastered the foster care system. I had dealt with the foster parents, their houses, the introductions, and of course, the good-byes. While most kids had parents, I had the State of Nebraska as my guardian, I was a ward of the state. But since the government didn't have hands and feet of their own, they thrust me into the care of various families and, of course, paid them for their trouble. I had seen several bad homes and a good one – Cheryl and Roger's, where I was given good food and clothes. They included me in their family. I was involved in pretty much everything the family did, even receiving birthday and Christmas presents.

I was always just the foster kid, but I knew about the wonders of adoption. I knew and understood that if a foster family felt that I was a part of the family, I could have been officially adopted into their family. Adoption! That was the ultimate success in the foster system. Like grafting a branch from one tree and inserting it into a completely different tree! The grafted branch lives and bears fruit as part of a new tree.

Occasionally, I wondered about my father. He had visited me that one time when he showed up with a smile on his face and a pipe in his mouth. As he puffed away he introduced himself and I remember the pleasant aroma of the tobacco. He gave me that toy and the coat with the ridiculous fur. Other than the few times I had spoken with my Dad, I rarely heard from him. I didn't have any updated information on where he was, or what he was doing. Was he remarried? Did he have other children? Even though he had signed away his rights, I didn't know or understand that at the time.

When he visited, he said, "Sara, you can come live with me."

I thought it would be fun. After all, he was my Dad! I was swept up in the emotion of being with my dad and said, "I'd love to live with you." That statement is one that I would regret many times over.

Meanwhile, my foster parents Cheryl and Roger were wonderful. Life was stable. I got along with Tracy like a sister. They had another baby while I was there, and named him Jerod. One evening, after I had been with them for four years, they sat me down at the kitchen table for a family meeting. With everybody present, Cheryl asked me, "Baby girl, how would you like it if we adopted you into our family?"

I screamed in delight!

It was glorious, a scene straight out of the movie "The Blindside." I was ecstatic. While they were certainly not rolling in dough like Daddy Warbucks, they were a good family.

I was loved.

I was accepted.

I had a home.

Cheryl and Roger met with Elise and started the paperwork right away. Elise filled them in on some of the process, "The state of Nebraska emphasizes the involvement of the birth parents in this process. It's a fair amount of legal proceedings but I don't think it will cause a big problem for you. Sara's mother is not an option. I know her well enough to speak on behalf of the state – she cannot adopt Sara. However, Sara's father is a bit of a wild card. He signed off his rights as a father when they divorced. But if he chooses, he would be able to adopt Sara."

Cheryl said, "Why do we have to involve him at all?"

Elise answered, "That's a good question. The state feels that the birth parents are the best option for kids in most situations. If the father expresses interest in adoption, then he can do it."

Roger inquired, "He has the right of first refusal?"

Elise said, "Essentially, yes. Let's keep our fingers crossed. I fully expect for the paperwork to go through and you'll be signing adoption paperwork within a few months."

Over the next few months, Elise made plenty of phone calls and sent out letters. Eventually she tracked down my father, Kenny, in Denver. She let Cheryl know that he had been found, and they were in the process of finalizing the paperwork.

Meanwhile, in Denver, I later learned from a trusted family friend that Dad had done well in his job and earned a handsome income. After his divorce he had undergone a vasectomy. Then he remarried, to a woman named Yvonne. There was some tension between the two of them: Yvonne wanted a child, but Dad couldn't provide that for her. When Yvonne heard about me, she convinced Dad to adopt to fulfill her wish for a child.

A few weeks later, which is forever in the life of a nine year old, Elise came to the house and sat down with all of us at the kitchen table. She said, "I've spoken with Kenny several times over the past two weeks."

Cheryl asked, "Did you get him to sign the paperwork?"

Elise sighed, "Well, he wants to adopt Sara."

Cheryl burst out, "What? That can't be right!"

I ran off to my room, hopped up on my bed, and cradled my favorite doll. The grown-ups talked through the legal system, while I escaped to solitude. I had long since cut her hair playing beauty shop, now I simply stroked her crew cut as I rocked back and forth on my bed. I sucked on my right middle and ring fingers. It was my bed. My doll. I thought about my family. They were my family. I looked at everything in my room. Cheryl had crocheted all my blankets and slippers. Everything there had her personal touch.

Why was I being taken away?

I crept back towards the living room and listened in on the conclusion of the conversation. Elise explained, "As a couple, they made the decision and we have set a court date to figure everything out."

I was stunned. *I wanted to stay. I had a home. I had brothers and sisters.*

I ran to Cheryl, climbed up on her lap, and said, "I want to stay with you."

She gave me an embrace that I remember as her trademark hug. I had a home for the past four years. I had security, and love. I had a family. I called her Momma Cheryl, and even to this day, forty years, I later still do.

I remember sitting in the courtroom. The wooden paneling was elegant and the chairs were soft and way too big for me. I looked around and saw everybody in my family in the room. I sat with Cheryl and Roger. Behind us was David, my brother from Jane's first marriage. He sat with his grandparents, who he was living with. In another area of the room was my sister Lisa, who had gone to live with another foster family. She sat with her foster mom. Yvonne and Dad were there up close to the judge.

I had no idea what they were talking about. My mother approached the front of the room and took the stand. I don't remember exactly what she said, but I do remember watching tears fill her eyes and pathetically flow down her cheeks. I wondered why she was crying. I was emotionally pushing her away because she had rejected me. Yet, her crying played on my heartstrings and I felt that she needed me. My brother and sister were visibly upset, they were mad at her.

I'm the only one who can reach out to her and give her comfort.

As the message began to sink in, I started to cry too. Between the two of us, we were probably too much of a disturbance for the small courtroom. Elise took me to a side room for the rest of the hearing. When I came out Mom was crying uncontrollably. I was allowed to hug her and she said she would see me soon.

Elise put a hand on my shoulder and told me it was time to let go. I held fast. I couldn't let go. Eventually she had to pry me away. My grip was too weak and I could feel my arms slipping from around her neck. I was screaming and kicking.

I want my Mommy.

I hated having to leave her out of fear of not knowing when I would see her again.

Across the room, Cheryl and Roger were crying. Their adoption plans had fallen into the abyss of the state judicial system.

Everyone was solemn. Sadness settled in the room like a heavy fog. Half the people were crying and the other half was stunned. There were only two people in the room who were happy, my dad and his new wife, Yvonne. They sat quietly in their seats with their winning grins.

What had I done wrong?

The judge declared that my mother had lost all custody rights. She was remanded to the state hospital. I didn't understand the depth of what had just taken place. When we got home, Cheryl told me that I was going to live with my Dad. I had a few days to let the idea settle in. In my simple understanding, I thought I would come back. I was sure that I'd continue to have good communication with Cheryl and the rest of my family.

The summer months had made the grass grow, a morning rain eased the midday heat. When the day came, I looked out the window and saw a beautiful butterscotch colored 1977 Lincoln Continental pull into the driveway. A slender man in a sport coat got out from the driver's side, and a blonde woman alighted from the passenger side.

Honestly, I don't remember packing my things but I do recall Dad putting my book bag and a few other odds and ends into the trunk. I gave Cheryl a big hug. Her tears moistened my shoulders.

She sobbed, "I love you baby girl!"

I tried to respond but she was hugging me so hard I could barely breathe, much less, formulate a proper response.

I had no way of knowing that it would be ten years until I would be able to hug her again or hear her say that she loved me.

I climbed into the fancy car and sat in the back seat. With my right hand, I held on to my purple afghan that Cheryl had made for me. In my left hand I clutched my hairless doll and I sucked on my fingers.

"Get your fingers out of your mouth!" Yvonne scolded.

I was shocked. I had always done that and had never been told not to. I removed my fingers and wiped them on the leather car seat.

"That's dirty and not at all lady-like."

I nodded and without thinking, quickly reinserted my fingers into my mouth.

She raised her voice, "What did I just tell you? Get your fingers out of your mouth!"

Why was she yelling at me?

Why was that wrong now, but it was fine yesterday?

As the miles droned on, Dad asked me "What's in your little bag?"

I told him it was my clothes and a few dolls. Nothing special. He looked at my shirt and pants and said, "We've got brand new clothes and a whole stack of toys for you at home."

We rode along in silence. By the time we arrived in Denver, I was emotionally exhausted. I wanted nothing more than to crawl into bed and be alone. But that was hardly the agenda that Dad and Yvonne had in mind.

When we finally arrived to his house, he pulled into the driveway and I saw a sign on their white picket fence that read, "Welcome Sara."

The house felt sterile, the carpet was perfectly vacuumed, shelves were ordered and the décor was impeccable. As I looked around I couldn't see any sign of life in the place. It was not kid friendly at all. Certainly not the blue Holly Hobby I was used to. It felt like a museum.

I asked, "Where are the other kids?"

He answered, "It's just you!"

Yvonne added, "Just the three of us."

I didn't know what to say, they just stared at me for an uncomfortably long period of time. It was obvious that neither of them had any experience with children. They had no idea what they were doing. I realized that I was still holding my bag. It contained my limited assortment of personal possessions. I dropped it on the floor.

Dad glared at me. I had no idea why. He looked at my bag on the floor, the back at me.

I asked him, "Can I see my room?"

"Sure" Yvonne said. She picked up my bag and happily led the way up the stairs past the first landing to a second short staircase and up to the second floor that held two bedrooms. Mine was on the right, Dad and Yvonne's was on the left. She opened the first door on the right and said, "Home sweet home."

My room was the size of my Cheryl's living room. The walls were old barn wood. There was a queen-sized bed, and a tall standing dresser in the corner made of dark wood with gold knobs. A shelf on the wall farthest from the door had toys on it. I walked over to it. There were no Barbie dolls or babies. Nothing I could dress up or play with. Yvonne looked on with an expectant grin.

I smiled politely.

Somehow, this was supposed to make me feel special.

Suddenly a black and white cocker spaniel sprinted around the corner and ran up to me. She jumped up on my legs and I reached down and gave her a big hug.

Dad said, "Meet Pandy, our other family member."

I loved her from moment I first saw her. She bounded into my arms and I carried her around my room. She ended up sleeping in my room every night. They gave me the chores of feeding and caring for her and I loved it. She was the best dog ever!

Yvonne gratefully left the two of us alone in the room. When she left, I crawled up on the bed and rocked myself back and forth. Pandy jumped up on the bed and sat next to me. I clutched my blanket and sucked on my fingers. I looked around the dark brown room. The rest of my possessions never made it to my room. I don't know what happened to them, but I never saw them again. My doll and all my other earthly possessions were gone. Even my Star Wars shirt disappeared after one trip to the washing machine. The only thing they allowed my to keep was my blanket, the purple afghan that Cheryl made for me. I still have it to this day.

My clothes were replaced. No longer was I allowed to wear halter-tops and pull-on shorts with elastic waistbands. I had to wear the clothes of their choosing.

I climbed up on the bed and cradled a pillow in my lap. I rocked back and forth wondering what life would be like living in a museum.

I arrived in July and they enrolled me into second grade in public school. During the subsequent months, I endured a series of changes. They cut my long blonde hair. My new look was short and cropped. Yvonne continually ordered me to stand up straight, and dug her knuckles in my back as a reminder. They made me stand differently, walk differently, essentially do everything I had ever done differently.

I missed Cheryl dearly. I had no idea that Cheryl had ever tried to contact me. Dad sent all of her letters back. I also never received any of the gifts she sent. I felt alone.

When they enrolled me in school for the first day of third grade, my dad introduced me with a new name. He told the teachers and everyone at the school that I was Ramie. Apparently, I suddenly had a different name. *Why?* I didn't know what he was doing. The other kids in the school questioned me about it, but I did my best to pawn it off like it was a clever new nickname.

That night, I disappeared in my room and tried to make sense of it. Yvonne approached me in disgust when I was sucking on my fingers. She commanded, "Give me your hand."

I held out my right hand. She took it and wrapped my fingers with the tape saying, "You need to stop sucking on your fingers."

I looked at her with astonishment. I looked down at my fingers, then back at her. I didn't dare say what was going through my mind:

What was wrong with the way I was?
My toys weren't good enough.
How I walked.
How I calmed myself down.
My hair.
My clothes.
Even my own name wasn't good enough for them.
Now you're saying I can't even comfort myself.

Yvonne left my room and I sat there in bed with tape on my fingers. I knew better than to remove the tape. That wouldn't be tolerated. Yvonne and Dad were systematically stripping me of everything that was mine. All that was left were parts of me that represented them. I realized that they were changing me into a new person, someone who they thought I should be rather than who I was. The problem was I wasn't a round peg and didn't fit into the round hole they were trying to force me into.

All that I knew was crumbling to the ground. My life had fallen down into itself like a building being destroyed with a mighty blast of TNT. One minute a sturdy building sits on the skyline, the next minute, there is nothing but a cloud of dust and debris. My life had come apart once again.

Chapter 3

I woke up the next morning with the tape still on my fingers. I dressed and went down to the kitchen and tried to eat breakfast. I removed the tape while Yvonne watched. I didn't make eye contact or protest. I just sat there, demonstrating that I had obeyed.

I ate and had an uneventful Saturday by myself while Yvonne cleaned the house. I promised myself to never suck my fingers again.

That night at bedtime, I rocked back and forth on my bed, without sucking my fingers. My private refuge was my room. The walls were dark wood, no pictures, posters, no favorite team, or band would ever grace those dark walls. Nothing would indicate that a child lived there. I was alone with my thoughts. *I missed Tracy and Cheryl. I wanted to spend a day playing.* As I rocked back and forth, the headboard banged against the wall.

Dad and Yvonne came into my room. Dad sat in an oversized chair, and Yvonne stood next to him, rubbing her belly. I didn't know it at the time, but Dad had his vasectomy reversed and Yvonne was pregnant.

Yvonne asked, "Why do you rock back and forth like that?"

I was puzzled, "What do you mean?"

Yvonne clarified, "You are rocking back and forth."

I looked down and realized that I was rocking. I stammered, "I don't know, I've always done it." It was the most natural action in the world to me. *Could this be wrong too?*

Dad said, "You really shouldn't do that."

I stopped moving.

Yvonne smiled, "There, that's better."

I was confused. *Comforting myself is wrong?*

She said, "Good night." And the two of them left the room and closed the door.

Only moments later, my rocking resumed and the headboard banged on the wall again. I had no idea that the headboard drummed out a rhythm that carried all around the house. I was completely unaware of the ruckus I was making.

Yvonne opened the door and stared at me. She asked, "What are you doing?"

I said, "Sleeping."

She replied, "No, you're rocking back and forth again. You need to stop that."

I closed my eyes and laid back.

A few minutes later, Dad entered the room and stood over me. I opened my eyes and saw his pipe dangling out of the side of his mouth. He shook his head. He said, "Let's try something new, this might help."

In his right hands, a pair of bungee cords wiggled like snakes. I had no idea what he was going to do with them. He proceeded to tuck the sheets in tight on both sides over my tiny frame. Then he laced the bungee cords from the right side of the bed to the left side over my midsection and my thighs. When he was done, I lay perfectly still. He stood up straight, inspecting his work.

Yvonne smiled and they both said, "Good night."

When they departed from the room, I wiggled and squirmed but was unable to get even a single arm free. The bed was like a straightjacket. My legs were fastened to the bed. I was stuck.

After a few hours, I came to the realization that I needed to go to the bathroom. I dared not call out. I held it. I wondered how long he would leave me tied up.

Would he release me later tonight?

Tomorrow?

I was supposed to go to church in the morning. Would he come in during the night and let me out so I could relieve myself? Finally, I had no choice but to pee. The sheets were soaked and the stench was horrible. I was secluded there, in the wet mattress all night long.

The following morning, Yvonne returned and released the bungee cords, one by one. The pressure on my arms and legs eased. There was no hugs or apologies after the events of the previous night. I rubbed my legs, they felt better without the restraints but the relief was short lived. The bedroom smelled of stale urine. When the stench hit her, and she saw that I had wet the bed, she screamed at me a series of insults reminiscent of a Marine Corps drill instructor.

She disappeared from my room and I sobbed. I was about to rock myself then remembered to stay still. She returned a few minutes later with a wooden spoon in her hand. She positioned me on my belly and she struck over and over again.

A few minutes later Dad came into the room and ordered, "Wash the sheets in the bathtub before we go to church."

The night of imprisonment had ended with an additional chore. After I washed the sheets in the bathroom and hung them over the railing, I put on my best clothes and accompanied them to Holly Park Four-Square church in Denver. I sat quietly in the pew next to Dad, while Yvonne played the organ. I stared at the orange carpet, and the orange cushions on the pews. We sang a few songs then Yvonne joined us as we sat together during the sermon. I looked around the sanctuary, there were anywhere between 100 and 150 people there in the building who all looked like perfectly dressed families.

I wondered, *Why is church always so boring?*

The small community of people was very polite but I felt alone in the midst of the crowd. Dad and Yvonne introduced me to pastor Gene and his wife Beth. I asked Yvonne, "Who is the piano lady?"

She said, "The lady who plays the piano?"

I said, "Ya."

She said, "That's Margaret Martin. Let me go find her so you can meet her." She slipped away and came back with two grown-ups and three children they were arranged like an Olan Mills photo. Yvonne announced, "This is Margaret and her husband Larry."

I waved.

"As you know, Margaret plays the piano, and Larry is a police officer in town. They are good friends of ours. And these are their three kids." She motioned to them with an outstretched arm. "Sherry and Ken are their biological children. And they also have Louis, who they adopted into their family."

Adopted! I'm not the only one who was adopted.

I shook their hands, not knowing what to expect. I got the feeling that everybody at church had a perfect family. Everybody was dressed so well and behaved perfectly.

Why did they like us? Did they know that I was tied up last night?

As we departed and drove home, my thoughts drifted to bedtime. I dreaded going to bed. *What would happen tonight?*

Dad and Yvonne knew that habits formed from routine, so he continued the routine of tying me to the bed every night with bungee cords. Every night I was tied so tightly that I couldn't wiggle free. Every night, I peed the bed. Yvonne considered my lack of bladder control as defiance. When she saw that the bed was wet in the morning, she spanked me with a wooden spoon. Occasionally, she broke a spoon on my derriere.

After a few nights, I learned to limit what I drank at dinner and afterwards. With a little planning, I could make it through the night without wetting the bed. In time, I learned to wiggle free and felt a sort of pride when I could make a trip to the bathroom. I slipped back into bed under the straps so they wouldn't discover my indiscretion.

After a few weeks, Yvonne came into my room at bedtime with a quilted vest in her hand. "I made this for you. I think it will help."

She presented me with the vest as if it were a special gift. I put it on. The large Velcro section on the back attached to the headboard. Unlike the dolls that Cheryl previously made, which were for my fun and comfort, Yvonne's vest was correctional in nature. She positioned me where she wanted me and I was fastened such that I couldn't sit up and rock, but at least I could turn over and take it off to go the bathroom.

I wore Yvonne's vest to bed every night. While I didn't welcome this new routine for bedtime, at least the bungee cords were gone. What did I learn from this series of events?

Comforting myself was wrong.

I was wrong.

Soon after this took place, Yvonne had her baby and named her Whitney. The baby took all of Yvonne's attention and I was grateful. Dad celebrated the growth of the family by purchasing a new house on the other side of town. It was a bigger and even more beautiful than the other house, with three levels, vaulted ceilings, and an elaborate kitchen. Mauve, flowery wallpaper covered the walls and a glass hallway table sat in the front entryway. Foot wide mirror strips stretched from floor to ceiling over the grey velvet wallpaper in the living room. It seemed that everywhere you looked there were more glass and mirrors. An oversized white fur chase lounge chair sat in the corner. The decor was vintage 1980s.

My bedroom was upstairs, within shouting distance of the kitchen. Dad and Yvonne's room was across the landing, far enough away that they wouldn't hear me rocking back and forth in my room. They bought me a new bedroom set with a roll-top desk and full-length standing mirror and white bedspread. The room was decorated with blue flowers.

Dad was proud of the new house, like a king in his palace. Clearly, he had made it in life! Of course, the place must be kept perfectly clean at all times.

After we moved in, Yvonne said, "You will keep this new house sparkling clean." She instructed me to roll the bedspread down to the bottom of the bed and use it as a decoration. I did as she said. I didn't use it as a blanket, but put it at the foot of the bed. During the night, I kicked it off the bed and it landed on the floor. The next day, when she found my white bedspread on the floor, she accused me of being disrespectful and took it away as a punishment.

Before the baby came along, Yvonne did all the cleaning, and the spanking. She maneuvered her wooden spoon with skill, like a professional baseball player wielded a bat. Once her attention shifted to caring for Whitney, both of those things changed. I was tasked with all the cleaning chores, and Dad took over as disciplinarian.

The first Saturday morning there in the new house, I woke up, with Pandy. I stroked her fur and she looked up at me. This little dog was my new best friend. She slept in bed with me and would listen to whatever I said. I looked in her eyes and wondered what we would do today.

Saturdays were fantastic! A day off. I enjoyed running around outside when the weather was good, or played inside and watched cartoons when it was too cold or rainy. I hadn't looked out the window yet, but I expected to play either inside or outside and I could be with Pandy. I reached over and gave her a big hug and she settled into my arms.

Yvonne broke through my bliss as she entered the room. She announced, "Saturday is cleaning day." She looked at me expecting a response.

I gave her a blank stare.

She continued, "Everything must be spotless." She gave a quick explanation of the vacuuming, dusting, and scrubbing duties, and suddenly I was on task. I started dusting at her command. Slowly, with the skill of a neophyte, I ran her dust rag over the surfaces of the desk and shelves. Yvonne instantly realized that I was not doing well and she showed me the dusting technique that she wanted me to do. Then she gave me the rag and I did my best to emulate everything she showed me. After the first task was complete, I learned her preferred method of scrubbing the baseboards, and cleaning the entire kitchen. She explained that when I was done, vacuuming the entire house was next on the list.

I would much rather have been outside with Pandy, but Yvonne would have none of that. After what seemed like forever, I finished vacuuming the downstairs and put the vacuum away, then reported back to Yvonne for my next chore. Yvonne saw that I had returned and she made a quick inspection of my work.

She pointed to the carpet and yelled, "What the hell do you call this?" The veins in her forehead bulged and there was fire in her eyes. She stood with me on the outside of the living area, arms crossed over her chest. Mine lay idle at my side. I scanned the room, the precious décor was all in place, the carpet was vacuumed. I had no idea what she was upset about.

I wondered, *It's been vacuumed clean. Is she talking about the shelves on the wall? I dusted everything. What is she upset about?*

I shrugged in silence.

Finally she said, "It looks horrible!"

I was confused, "What does?"

She walked to the middle of the room and pointed at the carpet. "The vacuum lines need to be straight. Ms and Ws. Straight, make it look like you meant to actually clean the room."

My eyebrows raised and my forehead wrinkled. I didn't see the purpose of writing obscure letters in the carpet. I had done the job and made it clean. Now I just wanted to go to my room to escape her wrath. I nodded.

"Do it again," she commanded. "When the lines are done, don't walk on the carpet. Leave it pristine, clean. It should look like it has been cleaned."

I plugged the vacuum in and attempted to redraw the letters in the carpet. She watched as I struggled. Using two hands on the skinny handle, I lumbered the machine back and forth yet my calligraphy was nothing like the experienced hand of a grown-up. She watched as I wrote lines that ended up crooked and meaningless. She disappeared into the kitchen. I was thankful she left, but when she returned with a wooden spoon in her hand, my heart sank.

"It's obvious that you aren't even trying." Then she ordered, "Go to your room."

I obeyed and marched up the stairs. She followed me up into my room and made me lay on the bed. She swung and connected with my hind end. Pain seared through my body as I tried to process what was going on. Instinctively, I covered my butt with my hands. *Surely that would protect me from being hit again.* My knuckles took the next blow. That hurt worse than the first hit! I moved my hands and the subsequent blows were a blur. She eventually stopped. My butt and hands throbbed. I lay on the bed crying.

"Follow me," she commanded. She led the way back downstairs and retrieved the vacuum. She quickly plugged it in and moved into position. She looked at me and said, "Watch."

She vacuumed the carpet. Her strong adult arm maneuvered the machine back and forth with practiced ease. A step forward, pushing the Hoover to the wall, a step back, bringing it back. She motioned to the floor. Perfect Ms and Ws.

She sneered, "Do you see this?"

I nodded.

"I think you've learned something, am I right?"

I stared at the Ms and Ws and nodded. Inside, I was thinking, *The only thing I can learn from this experience is that she vacuums letters, and I just cleaned the carpet.*

I cleaned and washed all day. It was easily the longest amount of time I had ever spent working. At the end of the day, my shoulders and back ached but the work was far from over. After dinner I was instructed to clean the kitchen and make it spotless. Yvonne instructed me on the "proper" way of cleaning the kitchen. On the countertops sat a number of grey decorative canisters labeled "Sugar", "Flour", and "Coffee." As part of cleaning the countertop, each of these needed to be picked up sprayed with the kitchen cleaner spray and wiped down. The counter underneath must also be sprayed and wiped clean all the way back to the corners. This had to be done every time the kitchen was cleaned, even if it looked fine. The dishes needed to be cleaned thoroughly then put into the dishwasher. The coffee pot needed to be cleaned and free of soapsuds. Everything needed to be spotless.

I received my marching orders and worked on the kitchen. It was late in the evening when Yvonne finally gave her approval. I escaped to my room to be alone and quickly fell asleep.

The house always looked like it was ready for a magazine photo shoot, I learned to make perfect vacuum lines on the carpet, and nothing in the house was out of place. Saturdays became cleaning marathons, and even when I was practiced and skilled at cleaning, it took me all day to vacuum, dust every inch of the décor, and scrub down every counter top.

A couple of months later, I was fast asleep in my bedroom on a Saturday night when they returned from an evening out. I woke to a voice in the kitchen, "Ramie get down here." The clock said midnight.

I wiped the sleep from my eyes and made my way downstairs.

Yvonne asked, "I thought you cleaned the kitchen."

I quickly thought, *All the counters were cleaned off, and the dishes were put in the dishwasher the kitchen was clean.* I replied, "I did."

Yvonne picked up the container labeled "Sugar" and pointed to a Cheeto sitting on the countertop. She growled, "If you cleaned the kitchen in the right way, explain this!"

I looked at the ground and said, "I guess I forgot to wipe behind them."

She scolded, "You didn't clean at all, did you?"

I stood like a statue.

She screamed, "Don't you ever lie to me!"

I got the right hand of justice across my face.

All the while thinking, *I didn't lie. The kitchen was clean. She tricked me by putting a Cheeto there.*

Yvonne said, "Why didn't you do it right the first time? Then you wouldn't have to be down here in the middle of the night. By the way, look at the dishes in the dishwasher. They weren't rinsed properly."

I re-cleaned the counters with Yvonne watching. With an exaggerated motion, I picked up each canister and wiped them down. I took the dishes out of the dishwasher, re-rinsed each one and dutifully replaced them into their position. I don't know what time I returned to bed, but the fear and adrenaline rush kept me from sleeping the rest of the night. All the while, all I could think was, *They are trying to make me someone that I'm not.*

Another time when Yvonne found deficiencies in my cleaning she asked, "Did you clean the kitchen?"

Whenever she asked a question like that, I always had a knot in the pit of my stomach. I tried to figure out what I had missed this time. I said, "Yes, of course."

She scolded, "You liar!"

I shrugged in defense.

Then she ordered, "Go to your room and write out 'I will not lie' on a piece of notebook paper, 500 times. Then come back here and clean the kitchen."

Reluctantly, I retreated to my room to start the busywork of writing out that I would not lie. I wrote for what seemed like hours. The punishment seemed unending. When I finally finished, I gave the papers to Yvonne and, once again, I cleaned the entire kitchen.

Dad was equally obsessed with the cleanliness of his personal realm in the house – the basement. It was as man cavy as possible. A roll top desk displayed his prized collection of car racing trophies. He wanted them perfectly dusted and was fastidious in the evaluation process. On the second Saturday in the new routine, I finished cleaning downstairs and he came down to inspect my work.

"Let's see how you did with the dusting," he said as he walked over to his trophies and reached to the back of the collection and picked one up. He ran his finger across the base of the trophy and saw a line of dust left.

He slapped me in the face and said, "You lied!"

He grabbed me by my wrists and pinned me against the wall, then threw me to the floor. I felt a crack from my right wrist as I hit the ground. Once I was on the floor, he delivered a swift kick in the ribs that lifted me off the ground and sent me tumbling across the room.

I winced in pain, "I'm sorry. I'll clean it again."

"If you had done it right the first time, this wouldn't happen."

I struggled to my feet. "I'll do it right now."

He left. I knew he would be back soon. I had to work swiftly. I removed the trophies one by one and cleaned the desktop. Then I cleaned each trophy one by one. All the while I thought about Dad's punishments. He had hit, slapped, and kicked me for the slightest infractions. As long as I wore long pants and a tee shirt, my bruises didn't show. He was skilled at avoiding my arms and face. He only caused damage that didn't show. I considered the creative times when I cursed or used language they found unfit. They washed my mouth out with soap. If someone could see the hidden parts, they would see into my soul. My body was beaten so often that anyone would know I was abused. Yet, Dad continued to expect me to conform to fit their idea of an ideal child. The lies and cover-up were just another routine.

When he returned to inspect the basement once again, it was spotless. There was no, "Thank you." He didn't commend me with a statement like "Good job" or "Well done." I came to never expect anything remotely positive. The words "I love you" would never be directed towards me.

I was a somber child and almost never smiled. The battery at home was overwrought with a continual battle to cover it up at school. On Sunday, church was another time to pretend that I was happy. For my parents, they got to see their friends, and gave the "perfect family picture" of our existence.

The one person I enjoyed seeing was Margaret, the piano lady. I peeked at her through the raised piano lid and saw her eyes. She smiled at me and I couldn't help but smile. It was our own little secret!

Dad and Yvonne did their level best to promote the image of a happy family. Nobody knew the turmoil that happened behind closed doors. The Olin Mills version of the Smith family is all anyone could see from the outside. In fact, this photo, where Whitney is a baby on Yvonne's lap, is the last I know of representing a happy family.

Pastor Gene Applegate taught about being good. He used a few scriptures from the Bible and encouraged us to look our best. In his teaching he told us, "Christians are set free. Christians have been forgiven and live holy lives. You have to look a certain way. You have to act a certain way. You need to look good on the outside and that's what really matters. If you have problems in your life, it's from sin. You need to clean up your sin."

I didn't understand everything he was saying, but I certainly got the message. I needed to look good to everyone and when something went wrong, I was to stuff it deep down inside and never let anyone know.

Pastor Gene concluded, "You need to fix your problems and look like a Christian. Otherwise, you are in sin."

That was a simple message, but I didn't really understand it. Pastor Gene and his wife Beth were good friends with my parents and I got to be friends with Pastor Gene's daughter Lisa. I often spent time at her house and managed to sleep over whenever our parents allowed it. I was happy to escape the wrath of Dad's hand. Any chance to stay somewhere else was a welcomed respite.

A few times a year, Yvonne and Dad left for a week or so to travel on vacation. The first time they left Dad explained to me, "As a punishment for lying, you don't get to go on vacation with us."

I looked at my shoes. There was nothing I could say.

I saw that they were packing their bags and taking plenty of baby supplies – it was clear that Whitney was going with them. Apparently, she was good enough for them.

When they left, I stayed at Pastor Gene's house for the week. Pastor Gene's wife was an excellent cook and I enjoyed playing with Lisa. At bedtime, I was changing into my pajamas when Lisa saw the bruises on my legs and backside. She grabbed me by the arm and took a close look. I had variations of black and blue all up and down the front and back of my legs. Some were old and in the process of healing, many were brand new. My butt was also covered in bruising.

She looked me in the eyes and said, "Oh my gosh! What happened to you?"

I shrugged. *These are things we don't talk about.*

She stepped back and looked at all my bruising. In a moment of realization, she put a hand over her mouth and asked, "Did Yvonne do all of this to you?"

I looked around the room. *This is my pastor's house. If there was such a thing as a safe place where I could be honest and forthright, this had to be it. I'm supposed to fix my problems, so I should do that. I can talk with Lisa, Gene and Beth.*

I met her worried gaze, "Yes."

Tears formed in the corners of Lisa's eyes. She held my hands and said, "We're gonna do something about this." She called her mom to come into the room and said, "Mom, look at this!" She pointed at my bruises and said, "Yvonne is abusing her."

Beth bent down and looked me over and saw the bruises. She saw the front and back of my legs and everything on my hind end. Then she stood up and faced Lisa, "No, honey. Yvonne is not abusing her. She's providing discipline."

Lisa looked on in horror.

Beth turned her back to me and continued speaking to Lisa, "We just need to mind our own business. When we look good on the outside, that's all that matters."

Lisa looked at me apologetically.

Beth took a few steps toward the door then turned around and said, "You two finish getting ready for bed." She walked off.

I looked at the carpet.

Lisa said, "I'm sorry."

You should be able to confide with a pastor or his wife. They were teaming up with my parents. I should have never talked about my problems.

As I pulled my pajama pants on, I began to erect walls around myself for protection. This totally confirmed the teaching, "Don't say anything about your problems. Fix them on your own."

But for me, there was nobody to help and no way to fix my problems.

Chapter 4

Dad was a coffee aficionado. These were the days before Starbucks, and twenty types of Colombian beans at the local grocery store. It was simpler then, and he loved his coffee. Among the things that needed to be perfectly clean was his coffee pot. Every evening, I cleaned the kitchen as best I could. This included his precious coffee pot. As a thirteen-year-old, my attention to detail paled in comparison to his.

With Yvonne out running errands, I was home alone with Dad. He was tinkering in the garage while I cleaned. I tidied up the entire house including the kitchen. I washed his coffee pot and put it back on the coffee maker. He came in from the garage and went to make a pot of coffee. He held the coffee pot inches away from my face and screamed, "What the hell is this?"

He pointed to the line of bubbles that dripped down the inside of the pot and fell to the bottom. "What if I hadn't seen it and I drank from this pot? Are you trying to poison me?"

Poison? He's calling soap poison? They use soap in my mouth as punishment when I used foul language! This doesn't make any sense.

He carried on about how little I care about cleanliness and how inconsiderate I was. He repeated, "Are you trying to poison me?"

I was just cleaning the kitchen. How could I be accused of poisoning anyone?

He yelled and continued his flurry of accusations. I braced for a beating. I hunched over and brought my elbows together in front of my stomach, my hands over my face, instinctively protecting my most vulnerable parts. He bent over and opened the cabinet below the sink. He reached in and brought out a bottle of drain cleaner. He looked at it and nodded. Then he set the bottle on the counter in front of me.

I relaxed a bit. My hands slowly descended from my face but remained in front of me. It appeared that I wouldn't be beaten.

He yelled, "Do you want to know what its like to be poisoned?"

I was shocked. *Am I supposed to answer that question? No! The answer is NO! Nobody wants to know what it's like to be poisoned. That's obvious!* Yet I remained silent.

He handed me the bottle. I held it in front of me. It felt cold to the touch. I saw the label on the front of the bottle. It read:

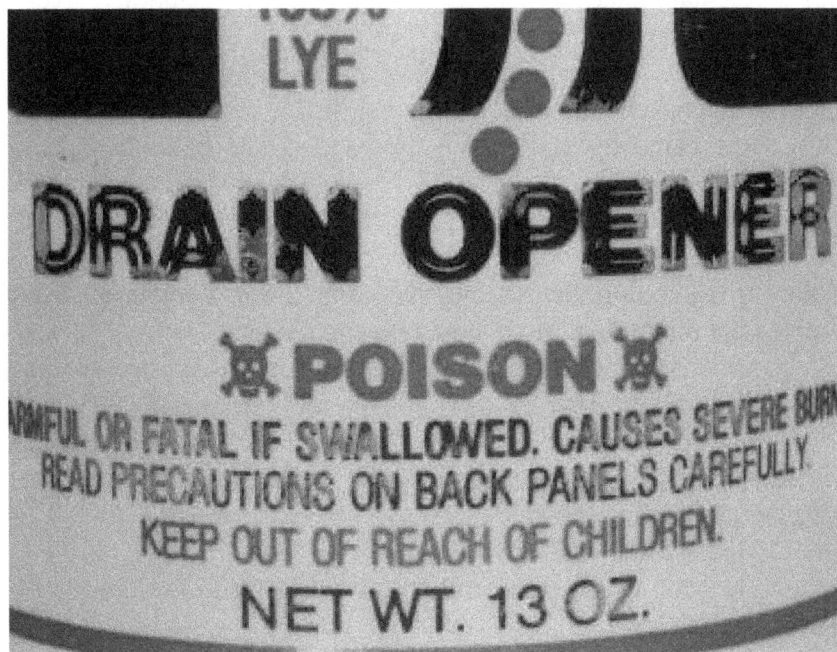

It was clearly something that I should not be allowed to touch, much less open and ingest. *Why is he showing me this?* The bottle shook in my hand as I trembled with fear.

He commanded, "Take a drink."

I stood there with the bottle in my hands, dumbfounded. *Is he serious? Is this some sort of test?*

My eyes said no.

He screamed, "You wanna know what it's like to be poisoned. I'll show you what it's like." He glared at me and said, "Drink."

I put the bottle to my lips and took a large gulp. I didn't dare take only a little. It tasted horrible. Then put it down on the countertop.

Dad corrected, "That's not where it goes."

I put the bottle back under the sink, I stood there looking at the floor.

Dad stormed off and went to the garage. I went up to my room. It seemed like time stood still. I had just taken a drink of the worst thing I could imagine. *What's going to happen to me? Will I die?* I felt nauseated. I went to the bathroom and huddled over the porcelain throne.

Yvonne came home a few minutes later. She heard me retching and asked Dad what was going on. He told her I was sick.

She came up and sat on the edge of the bathtub and asked what was going on.

I told her.

Her eyes grew wide. She didn't say anything for a minute. She looked at the ceiling, then at me, then at the floor. I could tell that she realized the magnitude of what he was capable of.

She whispered to herself, "He's going to have to answer for what he's done."

She patted me on the back of the head and went downstairs. I overheard her say, "You need to take her to the hospital. She needs to have her stomach pumped."

Dad agreed, "I'll do it."

He went to his room then came to the bathroom and got me. He said, "Let's go."

I sat shotgun as we drove to the hospital. I sat still, wondering what affect the chemicals were having inside my stomach. The concentrated sodium hydroxide had already burned my esophagus as I had swallowed it. If left alone, the toxic material would certainly kill me. A flurry of activity was going on in my stomach!

I said nothing and looked straight ahead.

Chapter 5

At Dad's the pantry was like a cornucopia overflowing with abundance of groceries, bought fresh on a regular basis. As a ten or eleven-year-old, I would get home from school, and grab a snack after school, then later that evening, eat a full dinner. My slender frame never showed a bit of it.

Gone were the days of culinary scarcity when I lived with my mother and we had to fend for ourselves day after day. In those long past days, it wasn't uncommon for us to go a long time without food, often days. My brother and sister found whatever they could to feed me, and without the two of them providing for me, I probably would've starved to death. I learned at an early age how to protect myself during lean times. My sister taught me how to sneak food when it was available, and save it for later. There were plenty of times that our secret stash was a lifesaver.

Later on, during my years in foster care, I continued sneaking food any time I could. Most evenings, I would stash part of my dinner in my pocket to save for later. Whenever I saw food that was left idle on the kitchen countertops, I stowed it in my pockets and either ate in secret, or added it to my stash. My pockets were continually lined with crumbs from little morsels I had grabbed. I never noticed if the other kids at Cheryl's house did this, it was just my normal way of doing things.

But at Dad's house, the mere presence of food was never a worry. Yvonne was a great cook. We would never stoop to the level of having simple foods like fish sticks or pop tarts. She made Italian food, Chinese cuisine, American classics, and more. Everything was the quality of restaurant food.

After living with them for about a year, I began to think of food as being always present and was happy to eat the high-quality meals she provided.

About the age of 12, Mother Nature's mid-childhood introduction of puberty changed everything. My outward appearance went through a series of ugly duckling stages and like any normal junior higher, I had a certain degree of self-consciousness about my appearance. I was average in both size and build. When I looked in the mirror, I saw an average girl in comparison to the other girls in school. I was neither heavy nor skinny.

This was quite different from how my father saw me, but he noticed every single change in me. But Dad saw it through a different lens. As I was standing in the kitchen he looked at my hips and said, "You're getting fat."

I didn't know what to say. I was offended, like any girl would be, but I dared not contradict him.

He went on to say, "I will never let you turn out to be a 'fat bitch' like your Mom."

He put me on a strict diet, and just like anything else in Dad's world he got his way. I ate nothing for breakfast and went to school. For lunch, I suffered through the minimal school lunch and came home with a grumbling belly. I couldn't think about anything except getting food. Dinner seemed to be a lifetime away.

But I had a secret weapon that had been instilled in my character from my early childhood – I knew how to sneak food. I grew up learning that particular skill, and now found ways to use it once again. This time, however, I performed the cuisine heist with the flair of a teenager. I waited until Dad was out of the kitchen and checked the fridge. Three big yogurt containers! *Perfect.* I looked closely at the configuration of the canisters and which direction each one faced. I grabbed all three containers, opened them and took a few bites from each. Then I carefully replaced the containers exactly how they originally were in the fridge.

I was always hungry, the meager diet that Dad mandated was insufficient. I stole from the pantry or countertop any chips, candy bars, or snacks that I could get my hands on. I was as stealthy as possible and made sure every container looked like it had never been touched. I made a stash in my room, but it never lasted long. I ate everything I stole within a day or two. I was pretty good at covering my tracks but I was in constant fear of my dad discovering what I had done.

Like most teenagers, I thought I was far better than I actually was. Soon, Dad found out that the yogurt was missing. I heard him holler from the kitchen while I was in my room, "Ramie, get down here."

A myriad of thoughts went through my head. *Did I miss a Cheeto behind the flour container again? Was my dusting of his trophies inadequate?* Then I felt a pit in my stomach. *Did he discover that I had stolen food?*

Hesitantly, I walked to the stairs and overlooked the scene. He stood in the kitchen with his arms crossed, like a drill sergeant disappointed in his troops. He pointed out the trio of yogurt containers. My heart sunk. I had been found out. I began to wonder what he would do and looked up at him as he struck my face with a clenched fist. I fell to the ground, bleeding from the corner of my mouth.

"You are not gonna end up a fatass like your mother."

I stayed on the ground hoping that he would walk away.

Eventually, after a series of denigrating phrases, I heard his footsteps fade off into the distance. After a few minutes, I started to return to my feet as he returned with a digital floor scale in his hands. He ordered me to stand on it. I stepped on the platform and stood still. The red digital numbers read out 132 pounds. I gave a sheepish smile knowing that this seemed like an acceptable weight for a 5'7" kid my age. (In fact, according to modern standards, 122 – 149 pounds is considered the ideal weight for my height).

He said, "115."

I raised my eyebrows and gave him a blank stare. I had no idea what he was talking about.

He laid out a new standard, "115 pounds, no more."

This time it was perfectly clear what he meant. I knew that I would be stepping on a scale again very soon and I had to weigh 115 pounds or there would be painful ramifications.

Over the next few days, I maintained his strict diet. The constant threat of his retribution overwhelmed my desire for food. I didn't cheat at all on his diet recommendations. Hunger took a back seat to fear.

After a week I got back on the scale and saw the dial register 122 pounds. I was thrilled. *I've been good, I have lost a lot of weight, I was on my way to his goal.*

When I looked up I saw his fist coming straight at my nose. He made contact and I saw a flash of white light. I fell to the floor.

"Defiant," he scowled. "Ungrateful," he hissed. "You are disgusting."

I looked up at him and realized that I was being defined as a number on the scale. An unrealistic number that set me up for failure every time.

Fat. I was too fat.

After a few minutes, I regained my position and stood next to him. He ordered me to go to my bedroom and showed up a minute later with a camera in his hands. He said, "Take off your clothes."

I hesitated. *This isn't right.*

I saw that he was serious and knew that if I refused, I'd be struck down again. I slowly removed my clothing and stood before him wearing only my underwear. He held the Polaroid camera up to his eye and took pictures of me.

"Turn and face the wall."

I turned ninety degrees and he continued taking photos.

I cringed in fear. *What is he doing? Why is he doing this?*

I dared not say anything.

I quickly got dressed while the photos began to reveal my imperfections. He showed them to me one by one. He pointed to my midsection and said, "Look here, all the pudgy fat on your hips."

The shame, humiliation, and self-hatred that I felt went rampant through my mind. He tossed the pictures on the floor and left the room. I picked them up and stowed them in my dresser. I wanted to throw them away, but I didn't dare.

That week I ate almost nothing during the day and lost a lot of weight.

Attention to my body had consumed me. I started seeing my body through my Dad's eyes. *I needed to be skinnier. I needed to eat less.*

So I did. I barely ate anything. The next time I stepped on the scale, it read 113 pounds.

Success.

It didn't take long for me to believe what Dad was telling me. My whole world involved him pounding me with the message that I was fat. Repetition of the lessons sunk in. If he said I was overweight and disgusting, than it must have been true. There certainly wasn't anyone else in my life telling me anything differently. On that subject he was the solitary voice that I heard over and over again.

He controlled my food intake as much as possible. I was hungry all the time. After a while my pelvic bones protruded. When I lay on my belly my hips hurt, I felt like I was balancing on my pelvis. I wasn't able to sleep on my stomach. I looked in the mirror. A skeleton of myself stood before me, yet all I saw was fat.

During the period of rapid weight loss, my strength was failing. I didn't have the ability to run, jump, and play, like the other girls. There were many days that I laid on my bed feeling like I didn't even have the strength to get up.

I sat on the edge of my bed at night and pondered my situation.

What possesses one human being to deny another human the right to thrive?

What drives a person to believe they have the power to deny another person food?

How far would I have to go physically and mentally to be good enough?

Somehow, I managed to dig deep within myself to keep going. I had to survive another day.

If I die, he wins.

In my weakened condition I had trouble making it through the day. In gym class while the teacher made us engage in normal exercise, I collapsed and hit the floor, unconscious. I woke up in the hospital where the doctor took one look at me and easily saw what I was doing. The doctor spent a little time asking me questions and they ran a few blood tests. They labeled me as an anorexia patient and the nurses scolded me.

They sent in mental health professionals who offered me help. Over and over again, they told me what I was doing was wrong. But I was convinced that it was right for me!

Eventually, Dad showed up at the hospital. He listened to the doctor say, "She has a severe eating disorder and needs to have long term counseling."

He acted shocked when he replied to the doctor, "I can't believe that! She's always been a sweet loving girl. I had no idea, nothing like this has ever happened before. I'll certainly talk to her, we'll get a counselor, we'll overcome this."

When we left the hospital and climbed in the car, the ride home was silent. After we crossed the threshold of our house, he yelled, "You ruined my day. I had to leave work and come all the way to the hospital to get you." He grabbed me by the wrists and threw me against a wall and I heard cracks and felt pain in my wrists and torso. I wondered, *was that me, or the wall that had fractured?* My wrists hurt for weeks.

The next day at school, I was called to the administration office. They had me sit in a counselor's office. The lady introduced herself and said she was willing to help. She placed a piece of paper on the desk and said, "This permission slip gives us permission to help you with everything you are going through. Take it home. Have your parents sign it. We'll get started right away."

I took the paper home, and gave it to Dad. He took it into his office and I never heard from him about it again.

The counselor saw me in the hallways during school and casually asked if I had gotten the paper signed so we could get started. I lied, "My dad is still thinking about it. I'll ask him again tonight."

Keeping up appearances was a normal part of our existence. By this time I was a skilled liar. I lied about what I had eaten. What my dad said to me. What he did. I learned how to lie in every situation. Of course, every lie required another lie to cover it up.

The second time I collapsed in school was in a hallway. Again, I woke up in the hospital. This time, I knew what to say. I denied everything and did whatever I could to keep the nurses from calling my Dad.

When my parents vacationed and left me with Pastor Gene and his wife Beth. I spent time with Lisa, but was shocked when Beth asked me to step on their scale. Dad apparently had instructed them to continue the regimen in his absence. I managed to sneak a couple of sugar packers while I was at their house and thought about how clever I was. But when Dad and Yvonne came home, Beth ratted me out and I was punished for stealing and lying. *I wasn't free to be myself anywhere.*

Once the weight loss had taken its toll, I stabilized at a meager weight and found a new normal. In time, I learned to sneak food and throw it up, fooling my body and mind into thinking that I had consumed calories. I learned on my own how to prevent passing out. I found that if I eat enough before gym class I'd burn it off and still have the energy to play.

Every time I took a bite of food somewhere inside me I heard a voice say, "Fatass." My own personal demon tortured me and this continued for years.

By the time I was in high school, my focus was continually on food, diet, weight, exercise and fat. I felt that I had complete control over my eating and went to great lengths to keep that control. I weighed myself on my own; no longer waiting for Dad. I weighed myself two or even three times a day. My father's obsession with my weight had become my own. Dad was certainly still involved. He purchased diet pills, laxatives, and anything else that I might need to tip the scale the right way.

At school I made friends with other girls who had similar obsessions. Once I had regained my energy, I earned a spot on the volleyball team. I found that these girls also struggled with eating and I enjoyed having a group that I fit in with. At lunchtime we sat together and ate. We enjoyed the normal gossip and laughed together, then we all went to the bathroom and threw up together. With all the girls in our little clique doing the same thing, it was easier for us each to continue to destroy ourselves. We had new ideas every day about how to justify what we were doing and we encouraged one another in our efforts. I learned to play the game and I played it well.

When I was at home, I generally tried to stay up in my room as much as I could. As long as I was quiet, nobody would bother me. Alone in my room, I would exercise for hours on end. I did sit-ups and push-ups, then I would go on long bike rides. Often, I would ride over to the nearby gas station just to buy snacks. I relished the sensation of chewing the tasty treats, then I quickly spit them out. Somehow this brought the satisfaction of having eaten something and made me feel like I had eaten a full meal yet starved my body of calories and nutrition.

I loved playing volleyball because it got me out of the house. It's a wonderful sport that requires quickness, teamwork, and skill. It's safe and most people get through a season without many injuries. When volleyball injuries occur, they are usually with fingers, wrist, and knees. I seemed to be the injury-prone member of my team. Since Dad had broken my wrists multiple times, I had all kinds of pre-existing conditions. My right hand had no feeling in the thumb area for years, yet pain shot up my arm constantly. Doing the set, bump and spike of volleyball was torture on my wrists. My coach helped by taping my wrists. That added stability and helped get me through practices and games. Soon I learned to tape them myself. I claimed that volleyball caused my injuries, finding another new and creative way to cover up my abuse.

I had reached a type of survival mode. It didn't matter anymore how I felt about myself. It didn't matter how skinny I got. It didn't matter how sick I was. It didn't matter what the doctors or anybody else said about me.

If I was skinny enough, then there was reprieve from Dad's punishment.

I was skinny so I was safe.

Chapter 6

Living in my Dad's house was a constant challenge. I was expected to live up to perfection and never knew when I would be punished, or for what reason. It always seemed that there was something that I had done wrong, and my dad was an expert at bringing down the hammer in horrible ways.

Pandy, the black and white cocker spaniel, was my Dad's dog when I arrived but she quickly became my dog. She greeted me at the door when I got home from school; she followed me everywhere around the house. We played together, and I spent lots of time with her. At about forty pounds, she was a challenge for me to carry, but she liked it. She slept on my bed and knew all my secrets. Everything that Yvonne or Dad did to me, I expressed to her each day. Her fur soaked up thousands of my tears as I buried my face in her side. That little dog was my best friend.

My dad felt it important to delegate responsibility to me and he gave me the job of taking care of her. In the mornings, I measured out her kibble and made sure her water dish never went dry. I let her out whenever she needed it. By the time I was thirteen she was far from her puppy years, and as an older dog, she needed to be let out frequently. I did my best, and truly cared about her. But every now and then, she had accidents in the house. To my Dad, this was

absolutely unacceptable and I could only imagine what wrath would descend from my dad if he found out. I did my best to clean them up immediately. I actually became quite skilled in removing pee and poop from tile and carpet.

One day Dad caught Pandy in the process of squatting down to pee on the carpet. He kicked her down two flights of stairs. I looked on helpless. There was nothing I could do.

In the autumn of 1983, on a beautiful Friday morning, I ran through my normal chores and patted Pandy on the head as I left for school. Some time during the day, she left a yellow stain on the carpet and Dad discovered it.

When I got home, Pandy greeted with energetic fervor as normal, but my father was far less enthusiastic. "Why did you do this?" He said, pointing at the pee stain. He hadn't cleaned it up, but left it as an object lesson for me.

I apologized and cleaned the mess.

Pandy's routine changed. When I got home I would let her out, but then 10-15 minutes later, she would need to go out again. She was having accidents far too often.

Dad protested, "I'm tired of this dog peeing on the floor, something needs to be done."

I had never owned or cared for an animal before, so everything was new to me. *Does she have a bladder infection?* I was hopeful that he would take her to the vet.

The following day, he found another yellow stain on the floor. He brought me over and yelled, "You obviously don't have any interest in taking care of this dog."

I scurried off to get cleaning supplies and countered, "She's old and needs more attention. I'll do better."

He said, "If you aren't going to take care of her, I will."

He grabbed the dog's leash and handed it to me. "Put her in the car."

I was ecstatic. *He's going to take her to the vet. She'll get some medicine and won't be having accidents anymore.*

I fastened the leash to her collar and led her out the front door to the car. Pandy loved car rides and was almost whimsical as she jumped in the back seat.

Without a word, he got in and started the vehicle. It was early Friday afternoon. *The vet would still be open for a few more hours.*

We drove down the block and into the center of town. Pandy happily jumped all around in the back seat. With the windows rolled down, she put her front paws on the door and hung her head out in the flowing breeze. She occasionally barked at cars as they zoomed past us. Her tongue flapped in the wind and the edges of her little mouth curled up in a canine style smile. She bounded from one window and back to the other over and over again.

I watched and tried to imagine what was going through her brain. *She's in her protective mode and she's trying to save us from the other passing cars and trucks.*

When we reached the veterinarian's office, we didn't pull into the parking lot, but rolled right on by. My heart sank. *If my dad wasn't taking her to the vet, what was he doing?* I had no idea where we were going, but I had a feeling it wouldn't be good. I considered asking what his plan was, but the rule was to never question him. I remained silent

I tried not to let my mind wander to the vile nature of his mind. *What would he do with my precious little dog?* She needed to be let out more often. Maybe we could have her stay in a kennel during the daytime.

He continued driving west until we were well out of town. The hills outside of Denver are exquisite in their beauty. On this day, I had no appreciation of the blue sky, glorious evergreens, and the world-class mountain range. I looked at my little dog and worried about what might be coming next.

He turned onto a dirt road and stopped in a secluded wooded area. He ordered me to get Pandy and get out of the car while he went to the trunk and pulled out a baseball bat. He slammed the trunk hard and marched toward me.

A baseball bat? Nothing good can come from that.

I froze and wanted to run. Where could I go? How can I get Pandy out of here? How can I protect her?

He snapped the leash out of my hand and secured it around the trunk of a pine tree. He turned and walked directly towards me, bat in hand. I had a gut wrenching feeling that he was going to hand me the bat.

What should I do?

Then suddenly he turned towards Pandy and swung the bat hard and cracked Pandy in the head. She yelped an agonizing cry and fell to the ground. Blood dripped from her scalp and she lay there helpless. Her body twitched.

I wanted to run over and help her. I wanted to protect her and care for her, but I knew there was nothing I could do. He beat her again, the blow of the bat making contact with her precious body. He swung a third time and her precious body lay on the dirt, limp and lifeless.

I was in shock and fear. I couldn't even cry.

Dad stood over the poor helpless dog like an executioner who took pride in his work.

I couldn't breathe.

After a moment, Dad ambled over to me and held the bat lazily as he walked. Then he pointed the end of bloody bat in my face and said, "Go get your dog."

I was paralyzed with fear. Somehow I managed to move one foot in front of the other and made my way over to the crime scene. I bent down and untied her from the tree. I kneeled down beside her and touched her fur. She wasn't breathing. I looked in her eyes but they didn't look back.

It wasn't natural to pick her up. Her weight was overbearing and I struggled to lift her lifeless body. She was warm and I felt her blood soaking my shirt.

I stood next to the car with her corpse in my arms. Dad opened the door and I manage to put Pandy's lifeless body in the front seat. I climbed in next to her and held her in my lap. Dad returned the bat to the trunk. I reached down and put her head on my lap and gave her a hug. I held her on the way back into town. I held her close and, hugging her continuously, I whispered to her, "I'm sorry."

I knew the rule of the house was to not show emotion. I tried to be stoic and hold back. I held onto my tears and refused to let them free. But as I held Pandy in my arms, eventually the dam broke and the tears flowed like a river down my cheeks.

Dad reached over and struck me with his right hand. The fury of his blow was like the crack of the bat on Pandy. His ring caught the edge of my eye. It stung. I could feel a trickle of blood start to run down my cheek into my mouth. I could taste the blood and felt the tissues around my eye starting to swell.

"Stop being a cry baby," he scolded.

I held my breath. If I don't breathe, maybe I won't cry. It failed. My tears dripped on her dirty, bloody fur.

He drove on, without any further discussion. I wanted to go home. I couldn't really think straight, but I thought that we could dig a hole in the backyard and have a little funeral ceremony for Pandy. She deserved it. She was such a wonderful dog. But with the situation the way it was, I could never ask Dad for anything.

At the edge of town, he pulled into a parking lot and stopped the car. I didn't know what he was doing or why we were there. He commanded, "Get out of the car."

I looked out the window and saw a solitary dumpster. There were no other cars around, no people mulling about. We were alone. Isolated. He told me to get out.

Surely he wants me to dispose of the body.

I slipped out of the front seat and stood on the pavement. I gently pulled her towards me, whispering, "Come on girl, let's go."

I picked her up and walked over to her final resting place. I whispered, "I love you Pandy."

I stood there as long as I could, holding onto her and repeating my adoration for her. The dumpster smelled horrible and the rusty steel railing was filthy and stained. I peeked inside and noticed that it was mostly empty, a horrible, dirty sarcophagus.

I looked back at my dog and thanked her for being my best friend. "I'm so sorry," I repeated.

Gravity began winning the battle and I couldn't support her weight any longer. I knew the time had come and I raised her to the railing. Dad blew the car horn. Startled and shocked, I jumped and almost dropped her. I mustered all the strength I had to lift her up and into the dumpster.

When I finally crested the top edge and she began her decent, I quickly pressed my hands over my ears so I wouldn't hear the thud of her body hitting the steel bottom of the dumpster. For a brief moment, I rested my head on the edge of the filthy railing and said, "Good-bye Pandy" one last time.

I looked at my shoes as I headed back to the car. I was devastated having just thrown away my best friend like a pile of garbage. The thought reverberated in my head.

I opened the door and sat down. Silence reigned the whole way home. Upon arrival at the house, I retreated to my room for the rest of the evening. I stayed there all day Saturday. Dad said that solitude would give me time to think about what I had done.

What I had done?

How could I think about what I had done, when he had just done what he had done?

He scolded me and told me that maybe next time I would take better care and pay more attention to my pets and not be so lazy.

I was forced to wallow in pity by myself and wasn't allowed to wash the blood off my hands or change my clothes. I lay on the floor dirty and smelly. I cried for hours.

Eventually, the grief turned towards anger. I started to think. My young mind processed everything that I had seen, heard, smelled, felt, and tasted. The images repeated themselves in my head over and over again. It was like a horror movie and I was in the middle of it. I looked at my hands, red with the blood of my beloved dog.

I realized that day that I officially hated my Dad. I never knew what he would punish me for and I hated the fact that I had to walk on eggshells every day. I remembered Cheryl's house where I was allowed to be a kid. I remembered having fun with Tracy and the other kids. But here, in this place, I was in prison. I hated that I never felt I could do anything right. I hated that I constantly had to conform to what they wanted me to be and wasn't able to be myself.

The following morning, I woke up and showered. I dressed for church and went downstairs. Dad and Yvonne were dressed in their Sunday best and we ate breakfast together. In silence, we drove to church as though nothing had ever happened. Dad and Yvonne greeted everybody with smiles and handshakes. I looked at my shoes and went to our normal seat. Yvonne sat down at the organ and led us in a Hymn. Margaret probably followed her weekly tradition and peeked through the piano lid to make eye contact, but I never looked up.

Pandy was never spoken of again.

Chapter 7

If you looked up the word "Grandma" in the dictionary, you would see a picture of my beautiful Grandma Elsie. She was my Dad's mom and was every bit the picture of the sweet old Granny. A petite woman, her red hair and blue eyes revealed the spunk with which she lived her life. Not a slave to fashion, she would never be seen without a polyester pantsuit. She ruled over the kitchen and always seemed to be in the process of making some type of food for the family. Her oyster stuffing was a family favorite. Thanksgiving and Christmas would not be complete without it. Yvonne picked up the recipe and made it to much acclaim. To this day, I still make Grandma's oyster stuffing on the holidays.

The summer after I moved to live with Dad in Denver, we took a road trip to visit her in Sioux City, Iowa. I remember her modest Midwestern house with wallpaper in the kitchen. Among the various Granny-style things at her house, there was one thing of interest to me as a young girl. Grandma had a photo album of my parent's wedding day. I loved looking through it and seeing the images of my mother. Tucked in the back of the photo album was a series of pictures of my mom holding me as a newborn. As a little girl, I loved sitting in the guest room in her house and looking at those photos. When Dad found out that I had been looking at them, suddenly the photo album disappeared.

I looked for it but couldn't find it. So I asked Grandma, "Where's Mom and Dad's wedding album?"

"Oh, I've wanted to hold onto that for you. I'll make sure you get it when you're older. Don't you worry one bit."

I was disappointed and couldn't help but think that she was covering for him. *Was she afraid of him too?*

Our visit was short but memorable. Several years later, we made the trek once again. At that point, she had retired from her career as a nurse and volunteered with the Shriners almost every day and managed to stay fairly busy.

On this visit, our social interactions seemed to be a little different. On the first day we were there, I was upstairs in the bedroom when I overheard her tell Dad, "Lock the front door."

He responded, "It's the middle of the day. Nobody is coming in here. We don't need to lock the door."

She repeated, "You're wrong about that. People come in and steal things from me all the time. Lock that door."

Dad laughed, "What do you have that they want?"

"I've had all kinds of things stolen from inside the house, even while I'm here. Last week, someone stole my car keys. It's not safe."

Dad asked, "They stole your car keys, but not your car?"

"Exactly!" She scoffed. "Who would do such a thing?"

Dad said, "Not a good thief. Listen, Mom, do you think you may have just lost your keys?"

"Absolutely not! Someone stole them."

Dad must have been frustrated with her, but I didn't hear any resolution to the conversation. A couple hours later, I made a visit to the restroom and the toilet wasn't working properly. I lifted the cover of the tank and peeked inside to see if something was wrong. I'm certainly not a plumber and I had no idea what I was looking at. The floater thing was connected to the drip thing, and there was no water in the tank. Obviously something wasn't working right. I looked a little closer and saw something shiny at the bottom of the tank. I reached in and pulled out Grandma's car keys.

Why are her car keys in the toilet tank?

When I showed my discovery to Dad, he let out a sigh. He knew that Grandma had a problem but he didn't want to deal with it.

I whispered, "Yesterday, I ran some errands with her. She utterly forgot where she was going. I had to reminde her that we were going to the grocery store three times."

He said, "She's never been confused like this before. Something is going on."

I added, "Twice she started driving down the wrong side of the road, I corrected her and she swerved back to the correct side."

He rolled his eyes.

I said, "Who knows how long she would have continued down the wrong side if I hadn't been in the car with her. Is she sick?"

He said, "I don't know. Maybe she's just confused. Possibly she has dementia."

I didn't know what that meant, but waited to ask anything further.

Dad took her to the doctor while we were there and they gave her the diagnosis of Alzheimer's disease. I didn't know about that at the time – I was just a sixteen-year-old kid – but she was already well into the second of the three stages of Alzheimer's. This is often the longest stage, where the loved one will require a greater level of care but will not recognize it. They may fight against those who are trying to help and they simply cannot take care of themselves. For Grandma, it could take years before the process progressed to the point of not recognizing herself or her own family members. Eventually, as she reached the third stage of this terrible debilitating disease, she wouldn't be able to feed herself or even communicate.

The moment Dad received the diagnosis, everything changed for Grandma, Dad, Yvonne, and myself. What it meant to her cerebral capacity, how her mind functioned, and how it would change over the coming years. Everything would be drastically different.

When Dad recognized the severity of Grandma's problem, he decided to move her from her home in Sioux City to his place in Denver. We helped her pack her house up and moved her. Grandma stayed in the basement bedroom of our house. We had plenty of room, so she really wasn't in the way. By all accounts, this was an honorable thing for my dad to do.

The church community congratulated him for being such a good son. We had a new Pastor named Joe Morlock. He had taken Pastor Gene's spot after he moved to Arizona. Pastor Joe was a big guy with short-cropped dark hair and big plastic-rimmed glasses. He was never seen without slacks and a button down shirt. He became a big influence in our lives. He was the type of guy that was comfortable with hospital visits and had a genuine peacemaker's heart.

I became friends with Pastor Joe's daughter who was a couple of years older than I was. Overall they were a great family. Pastor Joe approached my dad and said, "I think it's a great thing for you to bring your mother into your house. This will bring new challenges for you. If you need anything, don't hesitate to ask. I'll be happy to visit."

Dad smiled and brushed it off as if it was no big deal. At home, however, the atmosphere changed. As we unpacked her possessions and outfitted her room so that it felt like her own, I once again searched for Dad and Mom's wedding album. I looked through all the boxes but couldn't find it. I longed to see pictures of my mom as well as the photos of her holding me as a baby. As Dad and I unpacked her belongings, I sheepishly asked, "Do you know where your and Mom's wedding album is?"

Dad was quick to reply. "I don't know, keep looking. It must be in here somewhere."

I poured over her boxes one by one but never found the pictures that I desired so much. A family friend later informed me that when Dad knew that I was looking at them, he burned them.

We made a comfortable place for Grandma to stay and her room was filled with her decorations. I used to go down and sit on her bed and visit with her. As I went down to visit, I always crept down the staircase quietly in case she was sleeping. If she was awake, we would visit for a while. I discovered that while we chatted, she often thought she was back home in Sioux City. In the new house, Grandma was constantly confused. When she realized where she was, she wanted to go back home. I enjoyed our chats, but each time she got confused, she had a short fuse, and would be quite abrasive. With a gentle reassurance, I was usually able to comfort her and calm her down.

One evening, Dad, Grandma, and I were in the kitchen while Yvonne was making dinner. Grandma demanded, "I want to go back to Sioux City."

Dad spoke gently for a moment trying to calm her down.

In her confusion she screamed, "You're a liar. I don't live here. I want to go home."

He met her intensity with his own and yelled back, "You need to shut up!" He grabbed Grandma by the front of the neck and squeezed. Her eyes lit up with fear. Her slender neck was no match for the strength in his right hand. The veins in her neck bulged under the pressure. He stepped forward and thrust her backward. Her feet dragged along the ground until her body reached the wall and he pinned her there.

I screamed and ran to the other side of the room. Yvonne ran into the room and grabbed Dad by his hands. She looked him in the eye and pried his hands off Grandma's neck. As she peeled him off of her it was clear that Dad didn't have the patience to care for her. Yvonne had no solutions either. Living with Dad wasn't easy for her either. It seemed that all the women in the house were walking on eggshells.

Home was far from a peaceful existence. Whatever Dad did to Grandma and me, he most likely also did to Yvonne. Her life was tragic. Over time, a gulf grew between the two of them. He blamed her for everything. There was nothing she could do to make him happy.

When I was a senior in high school, they gave me a longer leash and I did my best to be out of the house the majority of the time, doing my own thing. I really didn't know much about what was going on between Yvonne and Dad. I heard occasional fighting behind closed doors in the evenings, but since I wasn't a part of it, I avoided their controversies like the plague.

Yvonne and Dad were good friends with another couple who lived just across the golf course from us, Sherman and Lori. They often came over to the house to play cards. Over time, Yvonne became good friends with Sherman. At one point, she confided to Sherman what it was like to live with Dad. I wasn't present in the conversation, but I can imagine that she shared some of the details of his temper and abusive nature. There were plenty of accounts to choose from.

Over time, Yvonne and Sherman became close friends, probably too close. On one occasion, Yvonne was crying and holding hands with Sherman. When Dad saw them he accused her of having an affair with Sherman. He blew up with a flurry of accusations and it ballooned into a Jerry Springer style drama. This went on for weeks, and all contact with Sherman and Lori were cut off.

I remember standing on the balcony upstairs overlooking the family room as Dad was yelling at Yvonne. I had no idea what they were yelling about, but I moved quickly to escape to my room. At the last second before I slipped into my chamber of solitude, I saw him pull out his gun and point it at her.

I slipped into my room and closed the door behind me. *Again with the gun! At least he's pointing that thing at her and not me this time.*

I heard Yvonne yell up to me in my room, "Ramie, call Pastor Joe."

I ran to the phone in my room and dialed Pastor Joe Morlock at his home. I had the number memorized, since I had called his daughter countless times.

Joe answered, "Hello."

I said, "Pastor Joe, this is Ramie. We need you over at our house right away. Dad and Yvonne are in a big fight and I'm afraid something bad is about to happen."

He answered, "I'll be right there."

Pastor Joe must have dropped everything he was doing and jumped in the car. Just a few minutes later I heard a knock on the door. Pastor Joe's presence brought a sense of peace to the chaos. While I hid in my room, he managed to calm Dad down and he prevented Dad from destroying everything around him. They spoke at length, and the gun was safely stowed. The screaming settled into normal voices and nobody was hurt that night.

In spite of the apparent calm, a vast chasm had been created in their relationship. Over the next few weeks, Pastor Joe offered his continued help, but little could be done for their crippled marriage. In May, they had gone their separate ways. After their divorce, I gave Dad a Bible. It was an expensive leather-bound edition. I didn't know much, but I hoped that he might somehow find answers in those precious pages.

In the three generations of my family prior to mine, none of the women had graduated from high school. Not my mother, grandmother, or great-grandmother. I was the first for a long time. This fact could have been celebrated, but Dad, going through his third divorce, wasn't up to celebrating much of anything. There was no party or celebration of any kind. He refused to acknowledge my mother, much less turn a negative into a positive for my sake.

That year I walked across the graduation stage and received my diploma without fanfare. I immediately started looking for another place to live. I couldn't wait to get out of Dad's house.

Chapter 8

Once I was freed from the chains restricting me to Dad's house, I couldn't leave that place fast enough. I was on my own and needed to start my own life. Chuck and Jan Callahan were friends from Holly Park Church. Their daughters, Kelli and Karla, were good friends of mine and they invited me to move into their home in Aurora, a suburb of Denver. I was thrilled to have a place to stay outside of Dad's house. At the age of eighteen, and out of his sight, I was no longer under the direction of his every word.

After living there a few days, I enjoyed my first free weekend without having to clean the house. It was amazing! Saturday was a free day, a day to have off work. Without a scrub brush, duster or vacuum cleaner in my hands. Nobody evaluated the Ms and Ws in the carpet to tell me I didn't do a good enough job cleaning. I was free.

I knew to never tell anyone about what happened at Dad's house. His discipline was off the menu of available conversation topics. Not that anybody ever asked about it, but there were a host of things I would never talk about – how he hit me, threw me across the room, broke my wrists, and pulled a gun on me. I dared not mention how he controlled my food intake, or what he called me. I tried not to think about how he treated Grandma. I buried these memories deep inside myself and knew how to lie about each and every one, to make my past look healthy and normal. I thought that if there were problems in my life, then I was a sinner. If it looked perfect and clean, then I was a Christian. As I enjoyed my Saturday, I tried to ignore the past.

The following day was equally amazing. My first Sunday outside Dad's house came with options. I could attend church if I chose to, or I could sleep in. The Callahans had switched churches and now attended Grace Community Church. I decided to go with them. I put on my Sunday best and followed them to church in my car.

The church was a converted office building. The service was a typical church service with a few songs, then the preaching, and an altar call at the end. Somewhere between 200 and 300 people attended and they all looked the part of the perfect Christian. I got to know a few of the younger people and started going to their youth activities. I mostly hung out with my friends and the youth leaders.

I looked for jobs in the paper and stumbled upon a couple of nanny positions. I had squeaked by to get a high school diploma and didn't have a lot of marketable skills, but I loved kids and knew how to care for them. After a few phone calls and interviews, I landed a full time nanny job for a lady named Teresa. She was a single mom living in Englewood (another Denver suburb) with a one-year-old daughter, Arianna, a beautiful chubby baby with brown hair and big brown eyes. I showed up at her house at eight in the morning and cared for Arianna all day.

Teresa was a property manager for an apartment complex. She worked with her best friend, Beth and told her about the arrangement we had made. Beth and her husband Steve had a three-month-old daughter named Sydney and they were looking for childcare. Before long, Beth brought her over to Teresa's apartment every morning and I watched them both. Sydney was a bald baby with blue eyes and the biggest smile ever! They were easy babies and I loved those girls as if they were my own. That was a perfect arrangement for us. They didn't pay me a lot, but it was enough to get by and I was able to care for both girls. After a few months, Teresa invited me to move in with her and I became a "live-in nanny."

Teresa and Beth took me in as part of the family and spoiled me rotten! I became like a family member in both families. During the day I was nanny Ramz to the girls. I was there for them every moment. I fed and changed them. I spent plenty of time in the rocking chair and put them down for their naps. I remember the day Sydney got her first teeth. I couldn't wait to report it to Beth when she picked her up.

Later on, Arianna began to babble. Then when she spoke her first word, I was there and told Teresa about it. She treasured the moment, and marked the day in Arianna's baby book. I loved every moment of being with those precious babies. When they rolled over for the first time, or began crawling, I was there and reported everything to Teresa and Beth.

In the evenings I learned a different side of life. Teresa and Beth held a huge party for the apartment complex at the apartment's clubhouse, just a short walk from Teresa's place. Beth handed me a red plastic cup and asked, "What do you like? Wine? Tequila? Beer?"

I answered, "I don't know, I've never had alcohol before."

Beth let out a squeal of delight! "She's never had a drink before! This girl is gonna have some fun tonight!"

They filled the cup with something and I took a sip. After a while, I took another one. As soon as I had made any progress on the drink, someone re-filled my cup. I have no idea what I had to drink that night, but I was a funny drunk. I laughed at everything and was having a great time. I was their entertainment and their big joke was to keep my cup full. All eyes were on me and they made sure my cup stayed full. For me, everything was new, and I imbibed everything they poured. At the end of the night, two of the girls that worked for Teresa and Beth carried me back to the apartment. I wasn't even walking. I didn't process what was going on, or think about what had transpired, I just collapsed in my room.

I woke up the next day and once again watched the babies. Caring for these kids was hard work. Lifting babies all day was hard work. I fed them, changed them, and had to deal with everything they threw at me, literally. As the shadows grew long toward the end of the day, my wrists hurt where the broken bones had never been splinted. My back let out an ache that reminded me of being kicked. The pain was a constant reminder of my Dad. I retreated to my room and rested, but my thoughts were never calm. My mind swirled around memories that I couldn't control. I hated the evenings and did what I could to not sit alone. I was in constant pain, both physical and emotional.

Some evenings I stayed at Teresa's and other nights I went to Beth and Steve's, but regardless of where I was, there was plenty of drinking going on. Teresa and Beth both loved Tequila. They had other drinks around, but it was mostly Tequila.

I drank through the evening and after a night of partying I would stumble to my room, numb from head to toe. I lay down on the bed and smiled. Something was different. I felt better. Then I noticed that I wasn't in pain. My wrists didn't scream out with every movement. My back was comfortable. I loved the new sensation.

Numb.

Then I realized that my thoughts and concerns had left my past in the distance. I no longer cared about what Dad or Yvonne thought. My food intake didn't matter. I could eat and not throw up. Somehow, for the first time that I could remember, what Dad and Yvonne said didn't seem to matter. I didn't even care about what they had done to me. I was mentally released from their stranglehold on my mind.

I was giddy. I was free. I was numb. I was drunk.

The freedom was only temporary. The following morning, however, reality struck. My body had searing pain, more than I had remembered. I needed an aspirin. I managed to shower and get ready for the day ahead and I spent the day with the babies. I picked up Sydney and winced in pain as my back and wrists cried out. All the while, Dad's words reverberated in my head.

It was just another day.

That evening, Teresa poured Tequila and I accepted. Once again, the pain dissipated with each sip. After a couple of drinks I was back to where I couldn't feel anything.

Numb.

I did my best to numb the pain. My back and wrists felt better as Dad and Yvonne disappeared into the distance.

That became my routine. The daytimes were filled with routine tasks, while my mind was tortured with memories. In the evenings I did what I could to escape.

Chapter 9

Meanwhile, I was getting to know a few girls from church. As much as I could, I hung around with my friends Wendy and Kelly. Wendy was 5' 6" with brown curly hair. We wore the same size and shared all of our clothes. After church we went to Taco Bell. We loved getting two tacos for a buck!

Kelly was the Callahan's daughter and she joined us in our escapades whenever she could.

I tried to see Wendy almost every night after work. This was far better than Tequila with Teresa and Beth. We found countless ways to have good clean fun.

Pastor Randy Scott ran The Grace Community Church youth ministry. Randy was a blast to be around, he was funny and we loved to tease him. As a big guy he drove a tiny two door Honda CRX. I called him the "Fat man in a little car."

Shortly after I got to know Wendy, we drove to Randy's house with a dozen rolls of toilet paper. We threw the TP up and over the trees, wrapped it around the bushes and even adorned the mailbox.

At the end of the adventure Wendy stepped back and admired her work. TP was draped all across the property – it was a total disaster. We loved it!

We went to Kelly Callahan's house and relaxed. Wendy looked at me and said, "What should we do tomorrow?"

I thought for a moment, "Fortunately, the church has a big youth group and there are three other youth leaders."

She smiled, "They have houses too!"

I went down the Rolodex of leaders and picked our next victim.

She clapped her hands together, "Yes! Tomorrow night, that is gonna get the greatest TP job ever."

We made our battle plans and realized that in that area, plenty of the neighbors would recognize our vehicles. Wendy said, "If you or I drive, then we'll get caught."

Kelly said, "I've got an idea. Since you two are staying the night, why don't we have my mom drive?"

I laughed. I jumped up and found Kelly's Mom, Jan in the kitchen. I made my proposal, "We need to go out and TP a house tomorrow night. If we drive, we'll get caught. Can you help us out?"

She smiled, "I'm an expert getaway driver."

The following night, Jan drove us to the grocery store where she patiently waited in the car while the two of us strolled in. We bought as much TP as we could carry. Then we went to Rick and Becky's house and threw the TP everywhere. Jan sat quietly in her vehicle and watched.

Jan rolled down her window and yelled, "You missed a spot on that bush over there!"

I looked to where she was pointing and saw that she was right. I ran over and used and entire roll on a single bush. With Jan's help, we made the whole yard look like a white out. Jan drove the get away car and we escaped without being found out.

That summer, no youth leader's house was safe. We TP'd all of their houses on a regular basis. Wendy used her cheap 35 mm camera and faithfully took pictures of everything we did to document our work. Afterwards, we got together at Taco Bell and shared stories. We told our friends about what we had done, but had to wait a week for the photos to come back with evidence of our delinquency.

I don't know if the youth leaders truly felt loved, or simply annoyed by us, but we certainly had fun. We got to know each of their cars well. We filled their cars with balloons, and wrapped them in saran wrap.

On one warm summer night, we went to the grocery store to buy TP, but my eye landed on a box of plastic forks. I picked it up and looked at Wendy.

"Yes!" She said. "How many are in the box?"

I read the package, "A hundred."

We bought a dozen boxes and drove over to Randy's house. One by one, we sunk the forks into the lawn, handle side down, until all 1200 forks were used up.

We took pictures then snuck away and laughed all the way back to Taco Bell. After we plopped down at our favorite table, I said, "They've been forked!"

The next day we covered a lawn with dish soap just before the sprinklers came on. The lawn bubbled up into a huge mess. Of course, everything we did was photographed and documented.

Wendy's dog loved to ride in the car but got carsick and threw up every time she went out. Wendy managed it well and would let the dog out to throw up. Of course, we took pictures. Eventually, we had an entire photo album of places where her dog had puked.

One night we drove around looking for something to do and ended up at Stapleton Airport. Wendy looked at the line of planes and said, "I wonder if we could get a picture inside the cockpit of an airplane."

We parked and wandered inside. In those days, there were no security checkpoints. We rode the flat escalator and ran into a uniformed pilot. We chatted with him for a bit.

He asked, "Why are you two out here this late at night?"

We laughed and said, "We just want a picture of an airplane. Can we get a photo of you inside your cockpit?"

He said, "Sure, I'm on my way now."

We were giddy. We followed him outside, across the tarmac and up in the 737. He took us to the front and showed us around. We took a handful of pictures, then thanked him.

We laughed all the way home and had plenty of stories for our friends at Taco Bell.

Taco Bell was centrally located, close to our houses and not far from the church, but the main reason we descended on the place is because it was cheap. Wendy and I made regular runs to eat tacos, burritos, tostadas, and other incredibly cheap meals. Often, our fourth meal! It was also the local hang out for most of our friends from church.

After a few months of drinking and eating fast food ... I gained weight to a healthy 175 pounds. I felt good and was okay eating what I wanted knowing I could and didn't have to answer for it. I also, on occasion, hung out with Kathie, a tall blonde with blue eyes.

Sitting across the table from me at Taco Bell, she said, "My brother is coming home in a few weeks."

I asked, "Home from where?"

She said, "He's in the Navy."

I shrugged.

"I'll introduce you. You'll get a kick out of him, he's a riot."

Two Sundays later, as I was sitting in church, I looked back over my shoulder at the entrance and in walks a tall, handsome, young man. His tight t-shirt bulged with muscles. He had brown eyes and brown hair, clean cut with a bleach blonde 3 inch "rat tail" at the back of his head! Our eyes met but we didn't talk with each other since the service was just starting.

After the service, up at the front of the church, he approached Pastor Randy, "I'm Chris, Kathie's brother."

Randy shook his hand, "Nice to meet you Chris."

Chris said, "Who is that girl in the back?"

Randy looked at the crowd of kids, "Which one?"

Chris clarified and pointed directly at me.

"Her name is Ramie, she's friends with your sister."

Chris declared, "I'm gonna marry her."

Randy chuckled and patted him on the back. He laughed, "Okay, whatever sailor."

After church we all went over to Taco Bell. Kathie plopped down next to me, "Ramie, this is Chris."

He smiled and sat across from us. He was cute and he knew it. As we dove into our tacos, Chris said, "Ramie, do you want to have a hair fight?"

I had no idea what he was talking about, but I said, "Sure."

"Great, let's do it." He said. He used a straw to make a little puddle of water in the middle of the table. He pointed at it and said, "Two pieces of hair will actually fight if you put them in there just right."

I furrowed my brow. "What? That doesn't make any sense!"

76

He quickly reached behind his head and snapped out a piece of hair and placed it in a puddle of water on the table. Then he motioned to me. It was my turn.

I picked a piece of hair and gave it a tug. Then set it in the water with his.

"Perfect!" He said. "Now watch close."

I leaned over and watched the two strands floating in the water. I looked up at him and was about to protest when he said, "Look closer!"

I leaned down close to see if the hair would really fight when he slammed his hand down in the water and splashed my face with water. He threw his head back and laughed.

I wiped my face off and laughed as well. Kathie could hardly control herself, she giggled like a little girl. We all had a good laugh but any amount of interest I may have had in him was now gone.

Despite my objections, Kathie gave him my phone number. After work the following day, the phone rang. I answered, "Hello."

"Ramie, it's Chris. Hey, we had a good time last night, I was wondering if you would be up for a movie some time."

"Sorry, I'm busy." I couldn't believe he was being so forward.

"Some other time, then?"

"Ya, sure." I lied. I hoped he would just leave me alone.

The following Friday the phone rang again, "Hello?"

"Hey Ramie, it's Chris."

"Okay."

"Are you busy tonight?"

"Ya, I'm getting together with some friends," I lied.

"Okay," he said. "If you…"

I hung up on him. *He must be a sailor – he is so stuck on himself!*

A few days later the phone rang again. "Hello?"

"Ramie, you really do need to get out and enjoy a night out."

I laughed. *He is persistent.* Yet, I declined.

The following day when the phone rang, I knew it was him.

"Hello Chris," I answered.

"You were expecting me," he said.

"You are predictable," I scolded.

"Why don't you take me up on my offer and find out?"

"Sure," I acquiesced. "If I go out with you, will you leave me alone?"

"I'll pick you up Friday night at 6:30."

"Sounds good," I hung up the phone and smiled.

He drove up to Teresa's house in his white 1990 Dodge Shadow. I welcomed him in and Teresa poured Tequila shots for all of us. After throwing a few back, we were off to a movie.

Afterwards, we talked late into the night. We talked about all kinds of things, except my past. I knew better than to bring up that type of topic — it only brought pain. Chris was certainly more than a simple-minded sailor. He was a caring deep young man.

Chris was quite willing to talk about his past. He was born in Renton, Washington then moved to the Denver area because of Kathie's allergies. He was raised in a solid middle class family. His Dad worked at Coors Bottling Company in Golden, Colorado and his mom stayed home.

After hearing about his family I teased him, "It sounds like you grew up in the classic Beaver Cleaver home."

He laughed it off. We talked late in to the night.

After we said "Good Night" that night, I looked forward to seeing him again. When the phone rang the following day, I answered, "Chris?"

I could sense the smile on the other end of the line.

We started talking and dating on a regular basis.

One evening Beth was having a party at her house. Alcohol was flowing and I had way too much very early in the evening. Chris called but I wasn't in any shape to do anything so I told him he could come over. I have no idea what happened, but apparently, I was drunk as a skunk and was in the middle of eating dinner. When Chris came by he found me passed out drunk in the bathtub with a cold pan of lasagna.

For some reason, he didn't take that as a warning sign that my life was more complicated than I was letting on. He didn't break up with me, or leave me.

He took the lasagna to the kitchen, and brought me a pillow and a blanket.

When we had been dating almost a year, our relationship was pretty well established and things were getting serious. We had a tremendous time together. Every time we talked on the phone, we connected on a deeper level. Each date was fun and exciting. Even a mundane date, like a walk in the nearby park, had an extra level of enthusiasm because I was with Chris. We kept active with the church and came along with most of their activities, together. And, of course, had some great make-out sessions. I was falling in love!

Chapter 10

Let's back up a little bit in the story. When I first moved out of Dad's house, he was left all alone with Grandma in his huge house. Without Yvonne around to tend to Grandma's needs, he soon realized that he was physically incapable of caring for her, and sent Grandma to live in an assisted living home.

All my life I had known Dad to be a wealthy man. He had always lived large. We always had a huge house, the best cars, and the best of every material thing. In retrospect, he spent more than he earned. Yvonne was also an accomplished shopper. She spent money like there was no tomorrow. When everything settled after his divorce, Dad was stripped of most of his possessions and his bank account was empty. Complicating matters, he also retired from his job. I don't know the details of why he stopped working, but after a career of spending and almost no saving, he had virtually nothing to show for all his work. His retirement income was a measly $1200 a month. He had never lived on so little. He couldn't afford to pay his own bills much less the cost of housing Grandma at the assisted living home. His options were limited.

Dad had traveled quite a bit in his younger years and was familiar with several small towns in Mexico. His language skills were adequate to have conversations south of the border and he was comfortable in Latin America. He knew that down there he would be able to purchase a reasonable home and live well. In fact, he would be considered a rich gringo, the status that he relished.

While I was working as a nanny, Dad sold his house and his remaining possessions and moved to the small town of Mulegé, in western Mexico, about half way down the vast desert of the Baja peninsula. Dad purchased a house and settled into the comfortable life as an ex-patriot living abroad. We kept in touch via mail. He occasionally sent me letters and I reluctantly read them, mostly hoping for updates on Grandma. He told me that he married a Mexican girl and let me know how Grandma was doing. After a while he sent a letter saying that he didn't know how much longer she had left, and that her mind was progressively failing. He explained that she could get around nimbly but often she didn't recognize him.

Half way through the letter, I put the handwritten note down and cried. I missed Grandma. I needed to see her. I needed to find a way to get down there and visit. I had no savings and couldn't afford to fly down there. Having taken no Spanish in high school, my language skills were limited to "Hola" and "Buenos días," yet I was determined to find a way to make it happen.

After a few moments, I composed myself and picked up the letter again. He droned on about things happening in town then he extended an offer to pay my way to come for a visit.

I managed to get the time off from my job and booked a flight to Mexico. The return flight was scheduled for two weeks later. With the ticket in hand, my thoughts were on Grandma.

I needed to see her. Would this be the last time I would see her? Would she recognize me?

My thoughts drifted to Dad. I wondered if a few months of retirement and being out of the United States would have been good for him. I reasoned that he might have made progress in his understanding of who I was. I would demonstrate for him that I had grown up and was no longer a disappointment to him. Surely he would want to make amends. *Maybe I would get an apology for all the years of abuse I received from him.*

The DC-9 touched down at Loreto airport where Dad greeted me. His new bride stayed home with Grandma. My expectations were through the roof. I was hoping to get some closure and peace of mind to get past the issues I had with him. We climbed into his yellow 1968 pickup and began the 76-mile ride North on the recently paved Highway 1 to Mulegé. Conversations were limited to small talk as we passed the desert sagebrush, various cinderblock buildings, and occasional broken down vehicles on the side of the road. Nearing the town, we turned off the Highway and drove on a long winding dirt road. The outlook changed from desolate brown prickly to a luscious green. Fruit bearing trees and inviting shrubbery covered the grounds. Birds nested in the trees and a small stream wound through the valley. It was a real life oasis within miles and miles of desert. The town of Mulegé was nothing to brag about, other than a place to live for a community that has been there for thousands of years. There was no tourism or signs of anything American. But it sat on a river where it entered the coast so it certainly had an element of rustic beauty.

We drove up a hill, out of the oasis back into the desert. Eventually we stopped at a large building at the top of the hill.

Dad smiled proudly, "Welcome to my new home."

I looked at the huge building and asked, "What is this place?"

"I bought it," he said proudly. "It used to be a restaurant. But had been converted into a house after it closed." Dad carried my suitcase inside. It was quiet inside and nobody was around for the time being so he gave me a quick tour. Ceramic tile covered the floors. There was a large living room and a restaurant-style kitchen with windows in every direction that revealed an amazing hilltop view. Up the stairs was a converted bedroom with a bathroom. Downstairs was a makeshift bedroom that looked like it used to be a storage room. He didn't have to explain, just like in Denver, the basement was Grandma's room. It was outfitted with a bed, dresser, nightstand, and the closet held her Polyester suits. There were no personal touches for grandma.

We went back upstairs and saw a pretty young Mexican gal in the living room. Dad introduced his new wife, Minerva. She was tall, thin, and she hung on Dad's every word. I gave her a cordial hug and over her shoulder I saw grandma! There she was, sitting in a chair in the corner. My beautiful grandma! While once a spunky, redheaded, petite go-getter she had been transformed into a frail remnant of what she had once been. She was thin, maybe 80 pounds. Her pantsuit covered her like a raincoat. Her disheveled hair had gone completely grey. Her once beautifully manicured nails were plain. She no longer wore makeup yet her big blue eyes still shined within her wrinkled face.

I sprang across the room and knelt down in front of her. My eyes begin to water. My heart hurt to see her in such a fragile, aged condition.

I looked at her and said, "Hi Grandma."

She looked back at me with a dazed look. There was a brief sparkle in her eye and I hoped that somewhere deep down inside her, she comprehended who I was. I placed my hands on hers and held for a moment.

She squeezed!

I jumped at the recognition and looked in her eyes. While there was no hint of recognition on her face, I convinced myself that she was confirming that she knew me. No words needed to be spoken.

Grandma was eating and talking just fine, even though she didn't always make sense. I simply enjoyed being with her.

The next few days were spent touring the run down town of Mulegé. The town was right out of a John Steinbeck novel. Dad played the role of the rich gringo and took me to the Mission Santa Rosaliade Mulegé, a simple but beautiful old mission that was worth the walk from town. One of the nuns that stayed there let us into the dormitory through a labyrinth of tunnels full of bird poop and up onto the roof. The view from the top was astounding. Other than that, Mulegé was little more than a dirty little town that Dad so proudly called his retirement home. It had nothing to offer in the way of entertainment.

I met his friends, did some shopping, and ate at his favorite places. I don't think I'll ever be a fan of turtle soup. When we were at Dad's house, things were different than usual. He had plenty of ideas for a leisurely retirement: fishing, drinking at the local taverns, and telling stories were his focus. However, taking care of grandma was not included among his list of things he wanted to be a part of.

When we got home from our outing, he saw grandma wandering around by the stairs. He grabbed her by the arm like a parent does with an unruly child, and forced her over to the couch. "Sit here," he commanded as he shoved her downward. She cried as she hit the firm cushions. She didn't look him in the eye, and was clearly afraid of him.

I thought about how this frail woman must have looked fifty years earlier. In here prime, she had been amazing! I imagined when she had been pregnant with my Dad. She carried him for nine months thinking about him, dreaming about what he would look like, hoping for the best for him. Then she gave birth to him and brought him into the world, wrapped in soft cotton blankets. He was just a baby. He didn't ask to be helpless, yet she cared for him in such a gentle, selfless manner. He was everything to her. As he grew, she cared for him like nothing else in the world mattered. She changed his diapers, fed him, and did everything she could to raise him in a healthy home.

Now, the tables had turned and she needed care. She was in this position at no fault of her own. She didn't ask for her mind to fail. She was just a frail old lady. She didn't want to have Alzheimer's disease. This was just part of life. He was there to give her care, but the love was not reciprocated. He had no respect or sympathy for her. He was not gentle, or selfless. It was as if he considered having her with him to be a punishment of some sort.

When we were hanging around at the house and Dad wasn't home, Grandma followed me around like a puppy. I loved it. I was careful to not go up or down stairs when she was following me. When I sat down on the couch she managed to nuzzle in next to me and grab my hand. She leaned her body into mine and rested her head on my shoulder. I put my arm around her and tried to comfort her as much as I could. She seemed calm and less agitated with me.

I wondered, *Is she silently asking me for help?*

During the daytime she was often very agitated. She wandered aimlessly through the large house and found Dad. She looked him in the eye and said, "I'd like to go home now."

"You live here now," Dad responded. "I've told you that a thousand times."

She screamed like a two-year-old child. She stomped her foot and said, "You're a liar. You are keeping me prisoner here."

Dad was getting rough with her and yelling, "Stop it, you don't know what you're talking about."

Dad's new wife didn't do much with grandma when Dad was home. I took her down to her room thinking laying down or a nap would help. She lay on the bed in her red and white polyester suit. I took a cold rag and sat with her, wiping the sweat off her forehead.

She calmed down after a half hour or so and laid there, whimpering like a child who had cried for too long. I climbed onto the other side of the bed and spooned behind her. I ran my fingers through her wispy grey hair. I watched every breath she took, I pondered back on all the accomplishments of her early life. She was funny, a joy to many. I smiled at this gift God had given to this world for 86 years. I lay with her and as the hours ticked by, she finally relaxed enough to fall asleep. As I lay with grandma I could hear Dad pacing the floor above me. He was raising his voice and cursing. I needed to go to the bathroom so I got up, walked to the side of the bed and kissed her on her forehead.

"I love you. I'll be right back," I whispered.

I made my way upstairs and to the bathroom. When I came out, Dad asked me where she was.

I told Dad that she was fine and resting peacefully. He looked me in my eyes and said, "Oh I'm going to make sure she stays resting peacefully."

I was in shock at his words and not sure if I had heard him correctly. I stammered, "What?"

He replied, "I can't do this anymore with her. Mentally, physically, financially – I just can't do it."

I was frozen in place. I couldn't move, words escaped me, I couldn't even cry. *Is he thinking of doing what I think he will? Is he that desperate? Would he go that far?*

He proceeded to go downstairs. I literally could not get my body to move, let alone wrap my mind around what was about to happen, or how it would transpire.

It seemed as if I stood there for hours, I was stunned. Really, it was only a few minutes. My body felt like I was stuck in cement and weighed 1000 pounds. Adrenaline finally kicked in and I ran downstairs. I reluctantly peeked around the doorframe into grandma's room. What I saw confirmed my worst fear.

Dad had his body straddled on top of grandma with a pillow over her face. He was pushing down with all his might. I could see her arms and legs flailing about. She was trying desperately to take in air. She needed oxygen, but he was too strong for her tiny body. After a few harrowing moments, her body went limp. Her fight was over and Dad had won. He went to dismount and our eyes met. I ran back upstairs and sat in a chair in the corner of the living room. I was numb. I wouldn't even cry. Dad had just murdered grandma in front of my own eyes!

I had no emotion left.

Dad marched upstairs and came into the living room. I saw him in the evening light and noticed an odd look of relief on his face. He picked up his pistol from the counter and came towards me. I was in too much shock to even comprehend what he was about to do.

He grabbed me by my ponytail and pulled back hard. He proceeded to stick the gun to my temple and said, "I know a lot of people here and I will get away with this if you don't say anything. If you do, you won't leave Mexico!"

He let go of my hair and walked away. He proceeded to step outside and make a phone call. About half an hour later, two men in street clothes showed up. Dad pointed downstairs and they disappeared into the basement. They returned with Grandma's body rolled up in blankets from her bed. I wasn't sure where they were taking her and couldn't pull the words together to even speak.

I watched out the window as the two men placed her in the back of their pick-up truck and drove down the bumpy dirt driveway. I could see her red polyester pants bouncing from under the blankets. Dad acted like nothing ever happened and went on with his daily routine. He let me sit in that chair for almost two days. I didn't eat. I didn't sleep. If I had to pee, I just went. I didn't even get up to go to the bathroom. I didn't care.

Dad told his wife, "Just leave her alone, she'll be fine."

I heard his words, Fine! *Did he really say that?*

I just watched my own father smother his own mother then stick a pistol to my head. Somehow, he thinks that I will be just fine!!

I did allow myself to cry some during the night. There was no amount of tears! Thoughts ran wild in my mind:

Did he kill her out of desperation?

Didn't have the financial means to take care of her or the patience.

Everyone ruined his life? My Mom. Yvonne. Me. Grandma.

What fueled his anger?

The day prior, she had been clinging to me like glue. *Was she asking for my help?*

Did she somehow know that this was going to happen?

Did she want me to protect her from him?

Did I let her down?
He told me what he was going to do and I didn't stop him.
Not only did I watch. I knew he was going to do it!
Even if I tried to stop him, could I have succeeded?
What would he have done to me?
I couldn't stop him
Am I just as guilty of murder as he is?
That makes me an accomplice to murder? (I thought that was true for the next 28 years).

Those questions would haunt me for years to come as I was forced to live in silence. There was no funeral and Grandma's name was never brought up again.

I didn't use a pillow again for many years.

．　．　．　．　．

Many years later, I found a picture of Grandma's house. Chris looked up the address online and found the real estate information on the house. We obtained the name of the owner – Amy and Brad. I contacted them through social media and told them that my Grandma had lived in their home many years before and asked for permission to visit the house. They were gracious enough to grant us access for a visit.

I remember stepping through the threshold and into her living room. As soon as I walked into the house, I fell apart. So many memories stormed into my mind, tears flowed down my cheeks. The house seemed much smaller than I remember, I suppose that's because I was bigger. The scent was different – each family seems to bring their own smell into a home – but the layout was the same. The carpet was new and the walls had fresh paint, but the kitchen was still grandmas' old kitchen. I stood at the stove where she whipped up dinner and closed my eyes. I imagined her zipping though the area wearing a red pantsuit. I walked down the hall and into the guest room where she kept that photo album and imagined leafing through the pictures of my mom holding me as a baby. I cried a lot as I remembered her.

We didn't stay long, but it was a meaningful and wonderful visit. It gave me a sense of closure after a long, hard journey.

I sat immobile in Dad's house in Mexico for a long time. I don't know how long. Minerva saw that something needed to be done and she finally helped me get cleaned up. With her help, I showered and into fresh clothes. She brought me into the kitchen and cooked some tamales and made a plate of fresh fruit. In motherly fashion, she encouraged me to eat. I picked at the food and moved it around my plate.

I still had another week at the house. I closed my eyes and did my best to bury my emotions. I shoved all the events of the past couple of days as far down into myself as I could and I went on.

I hoped for a quiet remainder of my visit. Dad had other plans, which would change my life forever.

Chapter 11

Dad and I went into town to run some errands and in the process of visiting the local stores, the locals offered their sympathy on the passing of his mother.

He said, "We'll go back to town tonight. Wear something nice."

I had no response. I retreated to my room. When evening came, he knocked on my door. "You ready?"

I didn't answer.

He opened the door and saw me lying on the bed, wearing the same thing I was wearing earlier in the afternoon. He spoke softly, "Let's go."

I wasn't interested. I wanted to go back home. But what could I do? I was in no position to oppose him. Never.

I followed him out the door and we climbed into his truck and went into town again. He pulled in front of the local restaurant. It doubled as a bar, and all-purpose local hangout.

Dad sat down on one side of the table, and I sat on the other. A local young man came up to the table and Dad welcomed him to join us. He sat next to Dad. We were not introduced and I never learned his name. He smiled and I did my best to be polite. Dad slipped him some money then stood up and looked at the guy and said, "Take good care of her now!" He excused himself and walked away. I heard his truck start and he drove off.

Great, I'm left alone with this young Mexican guy for the dinner.

The stranger nodded and smiled.

There wasn't much conversation going on as this guy didn't know any English and my Spanish left much to be desired. We ate and drank a heavy portion. When we left and climbed into his truck I assumed he was taking me home. A moment later, he placed his right hand on my leg, I pushed it off and sat in silence. *I'll be home soon and this nightmare will be over.*

He drove past the turn-off for Dad's house and kept going.

I said, "Hey! That was where we turn to go to my Dad's house."

He looked straight ahead and kept driving.

He put his hand on my leg again, and I repeated the rejection. I waved my hands back and forth and said, "No! Do not do that."

He kept driving straight ahead. I heard the locks click on the doors. I tried the handle, *Maybe I can jump out.* The door didn't budge. In my intoxicated state I started freaking out. The guy pulled over on a road at the end of a cemetery. He unlocked the doors and I instantly opened mine and jumped out and started running.

I knew what was about to happen.

I ran across the parking lot and headed back to the road. The dirt road was full of ruts and stones. I tripped over something and fell to the ground. He was in pursuit and quickly flipped me over and straddled me. He slapped me and ripped my shirt. He had my skirt pulled up and pinned me down until I stopped fighting. He kissed my neck and licked my chest.

He was much bigger and stronger than I was, but he hadn't had the emotionally toxic week that I had just experienced. As he sat up to undo his pants, rage welled up within me. A surge of adrenaline kicked in and I was able to get one of my legs free. I kicked his crotch as hard as I could. He fell over in pain and I stood up and sprinted. I ran for about five minutes before I turned and looked behind me to see if he was following. I was alone.

I stopped running and doubled over with my hands on my knees. After a few minutes, I began the long trek back to Dad's house. I'm not sure how far I had walked or even how I remembered the way. It was early morning by the time I got back to Dad's house. Nobody was awake and I came in without making a disturbance. I took off my torn clothes and threw them in the trash.

Then I proceeded to shower using an entire bottle of soap trying to wash off my attacker's saliva off my face and chest. I sat in the shower for a long time. After a while, I got out, dried off and got dressed. I lay awake the rest of the night.

I sat at the large kitchen table and overlooked the sunrise. It was not a welcoming sight. I didn't want another day to come. I just want to go back to my home in the states and carry on with my life. I had nobody to talk to and nobody to comfort me.

I heard some rustling in the kitchen and saw Dad making a pot of coffee. He tried to start a cheery conversation about my date. He asked, "Did you have fun?"

My mind swirled. I had so many thoughts I couldn't sort them out. *What could I say? If I admitted that he tried to rape me, would he be disappointed that he wasn't successful?*

I retreated to my skill of lying and said, "It was a good time."

Dad seemed puzzled. He went into the other room and made a phone call I could hear him getting irritated with the other person and caught only fragments of the conversation. I couldn't believe what I was hearing.

Did he set me up to get raped? Did he pay that boy to rape me? Did he figure that would make me forget about what he did to Grandma?

The next few days were a blur. Mentally, physically, and emotionally I was exhausted. Finally, on the day before my flight, the last day of my two-week "vacation" had come. I needed to give Dad the satisfaction of knowing I was doing well. I faked it well. We had a Mexican-style pig pit Bar-B-Que down on the beach. It was a whole town event. As usual I sat quietly not saying much due to the language barrier. Music played as people drank and danced and had a fabulous time. I decided to drown my sorrows and picked up a beer. At one point I noticed that Dad was having a private conversation with a young local fellow. They kept looking in my direction. I just figured Dad was keeping an eye on me. He certainly was.

When the sun had set and the bon fire coals were dying down people were mulling about. I sat on a log alone by the fire with a beer in my hand. Dad came over and sat next to me. He asked my why I was so ungrateful to him for setting me up with a 'good time'.

I replied, "I'm not ungrateful, I'm just tired and really not interested."

He slapped me hard and I fell to the ground. My beer flew in the fire and my knees hit the sand. I stayed on all fours for a moment. I could taste blood in my mouth and spit on the ground. Blood soaked into the sand. He leaned down and said, "You have always been an ungrateful defiant little bitch. You ruined me. I should have left you in Omaha."

Was he trying to ruin my life?

What had I done to him to make him this angry?

I stood up as Dad walked away. I needed to be alone so I walked a little ways down the beach to go to the bathroom. I found a spot in the shrubbery to relieve myself. As I pulled down my bikini bottom, someone grabbed me from behind and pulled me backwards. I fell back and hit my head on a rock. I blacked out for a few seconds. The man I had seen at the BBQ was now naked in front of me. He proceeded to try to get on top of me.

Are you kidding me? We have to do this again?

I laid there dazed with my head pounding. He grabbed my legs and pulled me towards him. As he did, I reached behind me, grabbed the rock I had hit my head on and sat up and slammed him in the head. He fell over and hit the ground. I got up. At that moment he grabbed me and pulled me back to the ground. I let out the loudest scream I could.

A few people close by came running. My attacker ran away and a girl helped me get my swimsuit and cover-up back on. She wiped the blood off my mouth left over from the blow that Dad had given me earlier. She walked me back to the crowd and sat me in a chair. I was stunned. Emotionless. The rest of the evening was nothing more than a blur. I don't remember going back to the house or going to bed. The next morning I packed my things and rode in silence all the way to the airport.

I will never return to Mexico again.

I thought about men. The way Mom dealt with men was a painful and distant memory. They were a means to get money to get high. As I pondered my Dad's relationships I saw that he ruined all of them. He had been through multiple divorces, each worse than the last.

I swore right then and there that I only wanted to marry once and never get divorced.

Not only that, but I would save myself for my husband.

We got to the airport, and I was anxious to separate myself from Dad. We stood in line and could see the plane a hundred yards away. It was just a short walk across the tarmac until I never need to see Dad again. As I stood in line with my ticket in my hand, I saw other family members all around. They were hugging and talking about their visits, recalling stories about things that happened. The airline worker announced that boarding was beginning and the line began to move.

There were emotional good-byes and smiles all around. Then I looked at Dad. He raised his shirt so I could see his pistol. I saw it and turned away.

Seriously! Like I need to see your gun to be afraid of you!

He said, "Remember what I said, if you tell anyone in the states I will make sure you take the blame and rot in jail the rest of your life."

I walked across the tarmac and boarded the plane. As I took my seat, I swore to myself that I would hold those secrets buried deep down inside for as long as he lived.

Chapter 12

Living at Teresa's house gave me plenty of flexibility. Other than my obligations to care for the kids, for 40 hours a week, I had the freedom to come and go as I wished. I even had my own phone number under my name at Teresa's house. (Cell phones weren't a reality yet).

One evening, when I went to my room before going out for the evening, I picked up the phone to check to see if I had any messages. I dialed the number and plugged in my code and the little voice announced that I had one message. I waited. Then I heard her voice, "Hey baby girl. It's your Momma. I've been looking for you and found your number through the help of an agency. I would love to talk with you but don't want to disrupt your life." She left her phone number and hung up.

I couldn't believe it. Her voice was instantly familiar. I dropped the phone and stood in shock.

I started to cry.

How I had longed all these years to hear her voice again.

Momma! That was really Momma Cheryl's voice in the answering machine.

I picked up the phone and dialed the number again. I listened to the message again. Then I listened again and again. I must have listened to it a thousand times that day. My excitement rose to the level I couldn't understand. Even through my excitement questions popped into my head:

Why didn't she contact me in the early years when she knew where I was? Was I just another foster kid to her? Why was she calling now?

My heart was swimming through a sea of emotions:

Happy to hear her voice.

Anxious to deal with the many questions of my past.

Anger over my Mom, and what she did.

Joy at the anticipation of calling her and talking.

I didn't call her back right away. I was excited but needed some time to process all of this.

The next day I picked up the phone and dialed her number. "Hello," the familiar voice came across the line.

"Momma Cheryl!" I stammered.

"Baby girl!" Her voice brought me comfort.

"Is it really you?"

"I've been looking for you for a long time now."

"I've missed you. How did you find me?"

"I found you with the help of an agency. They found that your name had been changed to Ramie. That was news to me. Then they tracked down the social security numbers for Sara Smith and Ramie Smith and found that they were the same. So it had to be you!"

We talked for a while and I told her the basics of where I was and what I was doing. I left out large chunks of my life, things that I never told anybody.

We talked on the phone on and off for a few weeks and wrote letters back and forth every day. (I still have all those letters and cards in a box). In one of our phone conversations, she gave an invitation, "I'd love it if you could come visit us for Thanksgiving."

I was ecstatic, "I'd love to!"

"I'll buy you a ticket."

After a pleasant conversation, we hung up. I had great hope and expectations of the upcoming trip. Teresa and Beth gave me the time off and I couldn't wait. She wrote me letters every day, telling me about various things that had transpired in her life.

Chris and I were in a flexible relationship, on again and off again. I didn't feel the need to talk to him about the visit. Wendy drove me to the airport. I was nervous and excited to go back to my past. While I never imagined that I would return back there again, I looked forward to walking off the plane and seeing Momma Cheryl's smiling face.

When I saw her for the first time, I squealed, "Momma Cheryl!"

She said, "Baby girl!"

I reached out and embraced her. How I had longed to feel that hug and hear her call me "Baby Girl" again!! We just kept hugging and crying for a long time. Cheryl was still the same as I remembered except her hair was a bit shorter. She seemed shorter and chunkier, but then again, I was bigger.

We pulled up in front of the same green house Elise and I had pulled up to sixteen years earlier. It still looked the same except the trees were considerably taller. She picked up a box from the trunk of the car and I did the same. We walked through the front door and I remembered the smell. The house was still the same, though it seemed smaller than I remembered. She walked me to the guest room and set the boxes down on the bed. It was the same room I had slept in all those years earlier. I felt like I was home.

Cheryl's kids, Tracy, Craig and Jerod, all still lived at home. They called me Sara. At first it took me by surprise, I'd been Ramie for so long. But I liked it, and while I was in Cheryl's house, I went back to being called Sara. Tracy was unwed and expecting a baby. Cheryl had a full house once again. I loved catching up with each of them. It was a joyous reunion.

In the evenings, Cheryl and I talked for hours. I loved listening to her tell me what she remembered about me as a kid. There were large gaps in my memory. She filled in those gaps with loving stories. She let me know who I was and that I was loved.

On Thanksgiving Day, I helped Cheryl in the kitchen. We made mashed potatoes, green beans, stuffing, and of course roasted a turkey. As we sat down to eat, I looked around the table and was truly thankful for my adopted family.

The following day Cheryl said, "I've saved something for you."

I asked, "What do you mean?"

She said, "Come sit here on the couch with me."

She brought out a box and opened it. Inside was a scrapbook from my childhood. Together, we flipped through and saw all the

96

pictures she had taken from the time I lived there. The pictures I had drawn in school were there. Report cards, my kindergarten diploma – she had kept all of it. My eyes were fixed on the icons from my childhood. Some of them I remembered, some I didn't, but everything was meaningful and special to me.

I couldn't thank Cheryl enough.

When the time for my visit had come to a close, I realized that it had only scratched the surface. I didn't want to leave, possibly because of the security I felt being back with Cheryl again. She always showed me genuine love. She was real. There was nothing fake about Cheryl.

Reluctantly, I boarded the crowded plane and flew back to Denver. When I got back from my visit, a friend picked me up from the airport and brought me back to Teresa's house. I arrived late in the evening and went right to bed. The following morning, as I got ready to watch the babies all day, Teresa said, "Welcome home. It will be another normal day for Arianna.

"I said, "I've missed her. We'll catch up today."

Then she said, "I've got something to tell you."

I said, "Okay."

She was blunt, "I've taken another job and decided to move."

I was shocked, "What?"

She said, "I'll be moving around Christmas time. We'll have to talk about what that means for you."

My first thought was, *I'll go live with Beth and Steve.*

Just then, Beth stormed through the front door with Sydney. She was visibly upset. She plopped down her baby bag and set Sydney on the floor.

Teresa asked her, "What's wrong?"

Beth replied, "Steve and I are getting divorced."

The two friends consoled one another. I picked up the babies and gave them space. The option of moving in with Beth was off the table. With a divorce, she wouldn't be able to afford a nanny anymore. What am I going to do?

After they left for the day, I picked up the phone and called Cheryl. I told her about the situation and that I'd have to find another job.

She said, "If there is nothing holding you there, why don't you just move back home?"

I asked, "You mean to Nebraska?"

I could feel her smile through the phone line, "Of course."

"To live with you again?"

"You can stay in your old room."

"You are so kind."

"There is always room for you in our house."

Through the day, I made plans. Moving would be easy, I had accumulated a few furniture items, but didn't have much. I thought about my friends and knew that, though I was having plenty of fun, I needed to move on.

My attention returned to Chris. We were having a great time together, but how could I tell him about my past? I realized that I had a lot of baggage I needed to deal with before I could move forward with my relationship with him. By going back, I might be able to get some questions answered about my past and find out who I am.

Chris and I had a brief conversation at a pizza place. I debriefed my visit to Nebraska. I told him about Momma Cheryl and how the memories poured in while I was there. Then I dropped the bomb about moving back there.

Disappointment showed on his face, "I can't stop you from moving."

I said, "I've got so many loose ends with my past. I just need to tie up a things before I can think about having a future with you."

He frowned.

I said, "We need to take a break. I'll move there and keep in touch."

He replied, "If it's meant to be, then you'll be back."

Just before Christmas, Momma Cheryl flew out to Denver and we rented a small U-Haul truck. She helped me pack up my bedroom set, a few chairs and some boxes – all my worldly possessions.

We spent the windshield time talking and catching up. I had so much to tell her and she wanted to hear every bit of it. She told me about all her other kids. I loved being with her.

Then she asked, "Have you considered seeing your mom again?"

I said, "Sure, I've wondered about it."

She confirmed, "You need to talk with your Mom."

I imagined the movies where Mom is the center of the family holding everything together. *Everyone depends on Mom. Mom is the best. What if my mom wasn't a drug addict? What would it be like to have a normal mom to go shopping with? To have lunch with? I know that I'll never have that, but I'm hoping she might be able to answer some questions for me. Having never had a real relationship with my mother, I feel left out. Incomplete.*

I answered Cheryl's question, "Would it be possible to resurrect some type of relationship with my mother?"

Cheryl smiled, "I hope so."

When we got to Omaha, Cheryl announced my arrival to the family. They all helped by grabbing my stuff and helping me move back into my old room. After Christmas, I landed a job at a day care at a church and met a great young lady named Becky. We spent all day together taking care of two-year-olds. We also spent time in the evenings together.

Cheryl made a series of phone calls to various connections that she had in the foster care system. We weren't sure what to expect as my mom had been in and out of the mental hospital all these years. This led her to find people who knew where she was living.

That night when I got home from work, Cheryl sat me down on the couch. She said, "I found her."

"My Mom?"

She nodded and showed me a slip of paper with a phone number and an address in the worst part of town.

"I'll call her tomorrow and set something up."

Cheryl found out that Mom was as normal as she could be considering her long history of drug addiction and mental illness. She invited Mom to Cheryl's house. I had no idea what to expect. I knew she wasn't Betty Crocker or June Cleaver but in my idealized mind, I hoped for the best.

When Cheryl brought her to the house, I was watching out the front window. She got out of the car, leaned against the front fender and smoked a cigarette before coming in the house. She looked like my mom – plump, larger than I remember. Her style was "frumpy" with baggy jeans and an oversized sweatshirt. She had a cigarette in her hands, no makeup, and her hair was unkempt and shorter than I remember. The effect of the drugs and life events had taken its toll on her outward appearance. She had clearly given up on caring what she looked like.

When she came inside, she gave me a hug. As we embraced, the familiar stench of cigarette smoke solidified her identity in my memory I knew she was my Mom. I was instantly comforted by her touch and her smell. I hugged her back but didn't cry. I didn't have much emotion. At that moment it didn't seem to matter what she looked like, smelled like, or even what she had been through. I noticed that I didn't fit like I used to. My body didn't conform to her rolls like it had many years ago when I was smaller.

As she sat down on the couch, the memories of the last time I saw her raced through my mind. She told me how much she missed me. She had been dreaming of this day for a long time. We shared stories and before she left, we exchanged phone numbers.

Over the next week I called a few times. Each conversation was short, but I felt we were making progress in reestablishing a long lost relationship. A couple of weeks later, we set up a visit at her apartment. Cheryl drove twenty-minutes across town and pulled up into the parking lot. The cars in the lot were older, run down, and rusty. The dumpster in the corner overflowed with a mattress and a couch sat next to it. All across the apartment complex, people sat on their front stoops, watching us get out of the car.

She welcomed Cheryl and I into her living space. I sat next to her on the couch and was almost giddy with expectation. We exchanged pleasantries then I began with my list of questions. "How old was I when I began to crawl?"

She squinted and thought for a moment. Finally she said, "I don't know."

I wasn't surprised. Not every event that I had with Arianna and Sydney was a landmark in their baby book. The joy of living those precious moments with the babies was fresh in my mind. I grinned, remembering Arianna as she wobbled through her first steps. Those times were so special to me, but I was just a nanny. Teresa's motherly heart treasured them so much more than I did. Surely my mother would remember.

I continued, "When did I take my first steps?"

She shook her head. There was a long pause. "I can't remember."

What? How can you not remember that?

I was shocked. I asked, "What was my first word?"

She responded, "I don't know."

I took a deep breath and wondered if she remembered anything about when I was a baby. I pressed in and asked another question, "When did I get teeth?"

She didn't have any answers. I sat back in the couch.

She either was never involved or never paid any attention to me as a baby. Her primary focus in life was finding her next high.

I was getting frustrated.

I wonder if she remembers any of the men that paid her for sex.

It's also possible that the years of drug use had scorched the memories I so desperately wanted.

Eventually she retaliated, "You kids drove me crazy. It was all three of you. I couldn't handle all the fighting. The demands. The constant cries 'Mommy Mommy!' The messes. You kids always needed something."

I was dumbfounded.

She continued, "With all of you around, I couldn't have a moment of peace."

I started to realize that she was not taking responsibility for what she did to us as kids. Instead, she was actually blaming us. She was claiming we drove her to abandon us. Somehow she found a way to lay blame on innocent children for her drug use.

I asked, "Was I a good baby?"

She finally remembered something, "No! You cried all the time. You drove me crazy, you just wouldn't shut up."

I looked at Cheryl for help. She reached out and held my hand, sensing that I was getting angry.

Mom asked, "Why are you asking me all these questions? Are you trying to make me feel stupid? I don't know the answers to your dumb questions."

I replied, "I'm not trying to make you feel bad. I'm just trying to know some simple things about when I was a baby. Most people's parents can tell them these things. Obviously, mine can't."

She looked at the carpet.

I sat in silence, fuming. This conversation was over. I had come to get help, but what she was saying was the opposite of help. In fact, I felt new pain. This was a real, distinct pain that I had never felt before. This woman, who I loved and longed for, actually blamed me for her drug-devastated life.

She blamed me!

I had no way of processing that.

Certainly, it couldn't be true. I was just a baby, and then a toddler. I was the one who should be cared for. It couldn't be my fault. It wasn't my fault.

When my mother laid the blame on me, it hurt. Deeply.

After a few weeks of thinking and processing what she had said, I started to realize that she did not have the mental capacity to care for anyone, not even herself. She had no way of being the mom I longed for and needed her to be. I called her briefly a few days later. During the conversation, I wasn't sure what frame of mind she would be in. I had to conclude we would never have a mother-daughter relationship of any kind. She was not capable of being a mom.

Chapter 13

I settled into a routine at Cheryl's house. I went to work at the daycare and spent time with my friend Becky in the evenings. I had come back to Nebraska for answers. I had questions, hundreds of them. There were so many things about my childhood that were a blur to me, situations that I didn't understand.

Why did I get adopted by Dad, not Cheryl?
Why didn't my mom fight for me?
What was going on in my mother's mind?

I wanted answers. I needed answers.

My conversations with my mom were a real setback for me. After those came to a halt, I looked to other venues for answers. I wondered if I could talk with my social worker Elise. Cheryl pointed me in the right direction and I made a few phone calls. With some effort, we tracked her down. Elise wasn't working in the same job anymore, but still had access to the system's files. We talked a couple of times on the phone and then met for coffee one afternoon. She agreed to dig out my case file. Over the next few days waiting for Elise to find my file, I wondered what could possibly be in that file. I tried to prepare myself for whatever I was going to read. What would I find? I was hopeful. *I want answers.*

I met Elise at her office and she greeted me warmly. She brought me to a small room with a heavy metal desk. She handed me a heavy white three-ring binder that was three and a half inches thick. I had to use both hands to hold it. On the cover was the title and logo of the social worker's office. I turned it and saw that my birth name was written on the spine, Sara Jan Smith. This was followed by large black lettering with my case number.

I'm a number, not a person.

"This is your file," Elise said. She gave me a hug, handed me a box of Kleenex and said, "Take your time. I'll be in the room next door if you need me."

I opened the file and looked at the first page. Legal sized yellow paper with hand written notes. I flipped through and saw white pages, and yellow. Thick pages and thin onion skin paper made up a collection of official looking paperwork. Most were mimeographed copies. Many of the pages had the police emblem in the upper right corner. *Could all these be police reports?*

There was no summary saying, "This is the story of Ramie." No introductory first paragraph. It wasn't a baby book with pictures of my first bottle, footprints, and recording of my first words. No description of my birth, or quotes from family members. There were no pictures of birthdays or family photos. Rather, it was a series of reports from social workers, police reports, and court documents, but they all included me somehow. This was far from a pretty story.

I sat down and began reading my file. I read a police report that talked about Mom's arrest for drug use, prostitution, and child endangerment. I flipped the page and saw psychology notes about my Mom. A few pages later, there were social worker notes on me at Cheryl's and with my mom on visits. It didn't seem to be in any type of order, just a collection of legal documents. I read about my childhood through the lens of law enforcement for four hours and went through the entire box of Kleenex. I was only half way through but I was physically and emotionally exhausted. I closed the binder and got up from the desk. I left the room in a daze and found Elise. I had no words.

She saw that I couldn't do any more that day and sat with me for a while. The following day, I returned to the office and, once again, sat down at the desk and read my file. Over the course of two days, I read about my first nine years of my life. I was emotionless for a few days trying to process my own life. I had searched for answers and found them in that horrible file.

Back at the house, Cheryl was busy with a new grandbaby. I considered reconnecting with my Mom, but she was in her own little fantasy world blaming me for her drug addiction and making her life worse.

Ramie, the girl who lived in Denver, seemed to be a different person than Sara, who was in Omaha. We were two different people that shared the same pain. I felt the hurt of rejection, being neglected, locked up in the trunk of a car, or in a basement. I remembered eating creamed corn from a can. I pondered the past twelve years with my dad and my thoughts drifted to Denver. I felt the broken bones that hadn't healed properly. I hurt everywhere, but mostly deep down inside.

Something has to change. I can't go on like this. I don't want to be that hurt, broken, neglected, abused little girl anymore!

I drove to a grocery store one evening. I bought a bottle of Tequila and some razor blades. I got back in my car drove over to the Missouri River. I parked on a bridge between Council Bluffs and Omaha overlooking the river and sat down on the pavement. I watched the cars go by and took a shot of Tequila. With each shot the pain lessoned in intensity. I don't know how long I sat there, but I downed the entire bottle. It effectively numbed the pain. But somehow, that night, numbing the pain wasn't enough anymore. I needed to end the pain.

I cried uncontrollably.

I opened one of the razor blades and held it in my right hand. I sunk the blade into my left wrist and brought it back. A diagonal red line appeared on the white skin. The cut was deep. I could see the tendons at the bottom of the wound before blood filled it and seeped over the edges. I could tell that it wasn't going to be enough and made a second attempt. This time, I dragged the blade straight across my wrist. I watched my tears fall from my eyes, dilute my blood as it ran down my wrist and soaked my pants. I'm not sure how long I sat there before I passed out.

I woke up and saw ceiling tiles above me. I was lying on a cold firm bed. I saw green tile walls and a green floor. *I'm in another hospital.* I have no idea how I got there.

I was familiar with hospitals. That's the place where you lie about the events that got you there in the first place. Then you put up with compassionate people doing things that hurt you while they insist that they are trying to help. They sewed up the cuts in my wrist.

After my mental fog settled down and I was able to give the nurses a phone number to call, Becky came and got me. She took me to her house and I spent the rest of the night there. The next day I sat at her kitchen table and processed what had transpired.

She asked, "Would you like me to take you back to Cheryl's today?"

I hadn't thought about Cheryl since before I picked up the Tequila. I shook my head, "No, I don't want to tell her about all of this."

She asked, "Why not?"

I lamented, "She thinks I'm having a great time here in Omaha. She's so happy to host me and has no idea what's really going on in my head right now."

Becky said, "You have to tell her."

I said, "Maybe later. Right now, I don't want her to see me like this."

After a few moments, she said, "Then you get to crash on my couch for as long as you like."

I was grateful for her help and hospitality and did just that.

I went through the motions of life for the next few weeks. Each morning when I awoke, I found a deeper sadness than the previous day.

I found ways to cover up my wrists at the church daycare and kept busy during the days, but in the evenings, the great sadness returned.

My depression continued to spiral deeper than ever. Nobody seemed to hear my cries for help or notice the pain in my eyes. If they did they either didn't care or didn't know what to do.

I heard the words inside my head:

You are worthless.

You are unfixable.

Nobody understands.

The paperwork from the hospital included the phone number for the suicide hotline. Sitting in the basement at Becky's house I dialed the number.

"Suicide hotline, how can I help you?"

"My name is Sara and I want to know what can be done to help a person like me."

"We have lots of things we can do to help. Can you tell me a little about yourself?" There was compassion in her voice.

I was in foreign territory. I didn't know how to ask for help. I had always been taught to avoid talking about my problems, covering everything up. I told her that I had slit my wrists. Then asked, "What do you do to help? If you commit yourself what do they do?"

She explained, "They evaluate you and do a psychological consultation. They decide if you are a candidate to stay and if you are then they treat you. You are welcome to leave whenever you want."

Thoughts of my mother swept over me. I knew about psychological hospitals with Electro Shock Therapy. I felt like I was becoming my mother. I didn't say anything for a long time. I felt incredibly alone. I certainly wasn't trying to explain what I had read in my file to anybody. There was no way they could understand.

She asked, "Do you understand what I'm telling you?"

I said, "Yes, but I'm not up for that." I decided in my mind that I wasn't going to go there.

She recommended, "You need to do this."

I thanked her for her help and hung up.

I had no framework for how to process the visits with my mom and everything I had read in my file. In retrospect, I was suffering from depression.

The voices reverberated in my head, for some reason they spoke in the second person.

You are worthless.

You are unfixable.

Nobody understands.

I had settled into a terrible new normal. From the moment my eyes opened in the morning, until long after they closed with my head on the mattress – I never used a pillow – the voices drowned me in a sea of negativity. I couldn't imagine that I was going through a diagnosable problem. It was just the way it was and there was no changing it.

I had always journaled what was going through my mind. That day, I made a journal entry expressing my deepest thoughts to nobody in particular:

Run

She has the eyes of innocence and the face of an angel. She has a tough exterior as if nothing could ever shake her most inner being. She is angry and hurt, yet she can't seem to grasp the words to express the whirlwind of chaos running through her mind. So she runs – what was going through her head that day? The anxiety, the fear, the adrenaline rush of the planned escape. Where was she going? What was she running from? What drives her to escape the pain so deep inside? What feeds this demon of destruction inside her? How far will she go to be free, to be accepted, to feel loved and to be called someone's little girl?

I went to the grocery store and bought another bottle of Tequila. Sitting in my car in the grocery store parking lot. I drank as much as I could. This time I held the razor blade in my left hand and dug deep into the skin on my right wrist. The blade sunk deep into the skin and blood oozed forth.

I waited, hoping for the pain to end.

I reclined the driver's seat and sat back.

This was the right thing to do, it was certainly the only thing that I could do.

The blood spilled over my arm, ran down my pants and pooled on the car's floor mat.

Becky spotted my car and opened the door. She was appalled at what she saw. She grabbed my wrist and held tightly, occluding the outflow of blood. She helped me to her car and took me to the hospital. This time I didn't black out.

They helped me walk through the sliding glass doors of the emergency room. As we approached the check in desk, the triage nurse stood up and helped us find our way past the waiting room and straight into the treatment area. I looked down and realized that I was covered with blood. The nurse brought us to the same room that I had been in the previous visit.

The doctor stopped the bleeding and sewed me up with speed and efficiency. While I was waiting for the nurse to place the bandage

108

and give the final instructions, I felt nauseous. The nurse wheeled me to the bathroom in a wheelchair and I threw up. I washed my face in the sink and looked in the mirror.

Who is this girl? How did she get to be this much of a mess?

The nurse wheeled me back to my room. She looked at me and said, "We don't feel sorry for people like you!"

Her words cut into my soul.

Everything I was saying to myself had been just confirmed by the very people that were supposed to help me.

There was no help.

Nobody cared.

Her words repeated in my head over and over again. I will never forget her saying that to me.

I settled on the understanding that this depression would be with me forever.

.   .   .   .   .

I went home with Becky and ended up just staying at her house for a few more weeks.

My thoughts drifted to Cheryl. I never would have done a suicide attempt at Cheryl's house. I wouldn't have hurt her like that.

Becky said, "You should call her."

I sighed, "I know." She handed me the phone and I dialed the number.

Cheryl's voice said, "Hello?"

I said, "I'm sorry I haven't called."

"Where have you been?" I could tell she was upset.

"I've had a lot to deal with."

"Let me help you!" She said.

"You don't understand. I came here for answers. But the answers I got from Mom, and from my file... I just can't handle it."

She retorted, "I don't understand what is so hard about being here. You have a home. You have food. You have everything you need. What is so hard?"

She obviously didn't see what I was going through. I said, "I've hit rock bottom."

We talked for a while. I didn't want to hurt her feelings, but it was clear she simply didn't understand where I was mentally or emotionally. She didn't tell me, but her adult kids were making her life far more complicated than I knew. She had a lot on her plate.

I was truly grateful for Cheryl. She had helped me find Elise, and my mother. She helped me get on the right path so that emotional healing could start. But it was a long road and I had no idea how long it would be. There wasn't anything further that she could do for me in that area of my life. They were my own demons. I had to fight them.

I sat back and looked out the window. The blustery wind blew the autumn leaves and I watched them fall to the ground. In a few weeks Chris would be coming to visit. I smiled in anticipation what that visit would be like.

Chapter 14

In December of 1992, Chris drove out to Omaha for a visit. A constant comedian, he played pranks and jokes at every turn and always made me laugh. On Christmas day, we exchanged gifts. I gave him a simple gift and he handed me a wrapped box. I opened it, inside there were several small other wrapped packages.

He looked at me, eyes wide with expectation and smiled, "Go ahead, open them."

Trying not to show any excitement, I opened the first one. It was a small, felt lined flip top box.

It's a ring! My heart leapt inside my chest. *Is he about to ask me to marry him?*

I opened it and inside was a plastic ring. Disappointment set in. I was half confused and partially upset.

What is he doing?

He replied, "It's not much, but it's all I could afford."

I glanced at the ring. It was the type of ring you get out of a little turn-style machine for a quarter. I chuckled, closed the box, and tossed it on the table.

"Open the next one," he said.

I reached into the box and pulled out a small wrapped rectangular package. Chris was grinning like a little boy on Christmas morning. I opened it and found a Reese's Peanut Butter cup.

At least he got this one right. My favorite candy.

I accepted the consolation prize, "Thanks."

He laughed hysterically then said, "Open it up."

I figured at least I would enjoy some chocolate and peanut butter.

He said, "You'll love it, I promise."

I looked at the candy. I knew Reese's Peanut Butter cups well, the chocolate cup, the ribbed exterior, and the treasured peanut butter inside. I could recognize this anywhere. I had my routine, I didn't pop the whole thing in my mouth because it was too big. I always ate the chocolate around the outside first, then I ate the middle.

However, this Reese's had been tampered with. Sunk into the middle was a solitaire diamond ring! I dug the ring out of the center and looked at it. It was covered in chocolate so I popped it in my mouth and sucked the chocolate off.

I looked back at Chris, his boyish expression was telling. He had taken a razor blade to the packaging and hidden the ring deep inside the chocolate. Then he had doctored the candy to look normal and resealed the package.

Suddenly, he was down on the floor on one knee.

My heart was racing.

I looked at him and smiled. He didn't say anything. He was just holding out his hands.

What are you doing? Why don't you ask me?

Then I realized that he needed the ring so he could ask the question. I spit the ring out into my hands, wiped it clean and handed it to him. He held it in front of him and proposed, "Will you marry me?"

I beamed, "Yes!"

While it might not have been the most romantic proposal, there was no walk in the sunset, or perfect date that culminated with a Hallmark moment, I certainly gave him points for creativity.

A couple of months later, he drove out to visit once again. We made tentative plans to get married. He helped me pack up my few things and took me back to Denver.

As we headed west on Interstate 80, Omaha was in the rear view mirror. I was determined to leave everything about my past there. I remembered that broken, unwanted little girl who spent years in that town. In my mind's eye, I pictured everything I had read in the reports. The memories were more than I could handle. The pain was unbearable. I was determined to make sure that all of that was going to stay in Omaha. I stuffed all of her pain down as deep as I could and vowed to never to let it come up ever again!

As we drove off together, we were no longer a couple of kids who were dating. We were going to be married! Chris was my fiancé, and I was his. It didn't take long for my mind to shift to a wedding. My wedding! Ever since I was a little girl, I wanted my fairy tale wedding. I remember playing with dolls where the boy doll waits at the front of the church while the beautiful bride floats down to meet him. Everything was perfect, the flowers were beautiful, the music was amazing, and of course the bride took everyone's breath away. I moved the dolls back and forth reenacting the ceremony over and over again.

As a little girl, I dreamed of a princess castle and feeling like Cinderella as she prepares to meet her prince. Now, it was no longer make-believe and I was free to plan our wedding however I wanted. There were no dolls, no make believe, it would be the real thing! I envisioned the perfect ceremony where I was the princess.

Chris' parents helped us reserve Lakewood First Assembly of God in Lakewood, Colorado. This would be the site for the rehearsal dinner, the formal ceremony, and the reception. I was excited to plan my wedding. Chris' mom and I went shopping for a dress and found a discontinued model that fit perfectly. It had a V-neck, poofy sleeves, fake pearls, and no veil. Exactly what I had hoped for. The fact that it was at a consignment store didn't detract from its perfect beauty. Chris' mom paid $100 for it.

As Chris and I made our plans, it was important to have all the pieces there. I considered Dad. Standing next to him would be awful. *Was it possible to not invite him? What if I let him stay in Mexico, an unwelcome persona non-grata?*

Then there was the rest of our family and friends. Nobody knew what he had put me through. Amazingly, everybody thought he was a good dad. It would be a seismic shift in the family dynamic to exclude him from the ceremony. To do so would mean that I would have to come out and tell everybody the truth about who he was, and what he had done. I refused to think of those memories. I was physically unable to speak about them publicly. I kept it stuffed down and hid the pain. I had to invite him.

I imagined him walking me down the aisle. The statement that a father/daughter couple at the back of a church make is rich with symbolism. He would extend his elbow to me and I would take it. He would guide me past the collection of our friends and family. This clear statement says to the world that he had cared for me, fed, clothed, and protected me for all these years. By walking me down the aisle, he proclaims to the world that he has been a good father. Lies. I was nauseated at the thought of him being there, but it had to be that way.

But that wasn't the end of the matter. At the front of the church everything would change. Chris would be there, too. As Dad handed me over, he would transfer all of that responsibility to Chris as he gave me away. This spark of hope got me through the planning stages.

Chris and I weren't perfect. My desire was to wait to have children but God honored my teenage wish to be my husband's first and we both lost our virginity together. Sadly, it was before marriage and I was pregnant. We knew we had been wrong, and repented. Then we met with Pastor Randy. He walked us through some things and encouraged us to move the date up.

Chris and I made our guest list and the wedding plans quickly came together. I called Dad in Mexico and extended an invitation to him. He arranged to be in town for a few days and gave me $300 to help with the wedding expenses. We also invited my Mom. In spite of the painful interactions I had with her, I wanted her to be there on my special day.

We kept the plans simple. Our plans included finger foods provided by friends, and a two-tier wedding cake. The day before, we adorned the church with blue and mauve decorations and flowers. We transformed a classic, traditional church into a beautiful cathedral where we would be joined in marriage. A friend of ours volunteered to sing the power ballad *Honestly* by the Christian rock band Stryper. (I still get teary eyes when I hear that song).

The rehearsal went off without any fanfare and the dinner was held in the church gym. Chris' mom served BBQ beef sandwiches and salads for everybody.

When the big day finally arrived, the piano rang out the tune, *Here Comes the Bride* with Margaret tickling the ivory keys. I held a bouquet of flowers in my hands as I walked down the aisle.

About 125 guests joined us for our celebration. As I walked down the middle of everything, I was the beautiful centerpiece. It was like I had imagined. I made eye contact with friends and family on both sides, smiles plastered on each of their faces. I looked ahead and saw Chris standing at the front of the church. The love of my life was uncharacteristically wearing a tuxedo. He and his groomsmen preferred jeans and flannel shirts. They looked like trained penguins as they squirmed uncomfortably in their white and black celebratory apparel.

I took Dad's elbow and step-by-step we made our way down the center of the church. Every step we took together was a lie. Clearly, he did not protect me. He did not love or care for me as he should have. He never once told me he loved me. He set me up to be raped, twice. There was the physical abuse. Every step was a painful reminder of who he was as a father. Deep down, I knew he did not deserve to have this honor of walking me down the center of the church.

But the lies were nothing new. Church was a place where we lied every Sunday. We had lied about our lives with our words and with our actions. I carefully covered the bruises and broken bones and we told everybody that we were doing well. In my white dress, I took each step in confidence of knowing that once we got to the front, he would give me away forever.

Each step I took with Dad was dreadful. My belly turned over and waves of nausea swept over me. Morning sickness. I couldn't tell what was making me sick, the baby inside me, or my nervous tension about the wedding. I was focused on Chris. I knew that in a few moments, I would be given away.

My mother was there too, sitting at the front of the church. Dad and I passed by her and the empty space next to her. She also didn't deserve the honor of sitting in that space. She was not a mother. She didn't have the capacity to be a mother. But it was my fairy tale wedding and I had invited her. She wore a flowered dress and filled her place in the ceremony.

We made it to the front and Pastor Randy said, "Who gives this woman to be married to this man?"

Dad said, "Her mother and I do."

He passed my hand to Chris and released me. He let me go and I stepped away from his presence.

He will never touch me again.

I stepped away from him for the last time, never to return. Chris stepped toward me and I met his gaze with a smile. His face was hazy through tears that went far beyond the joy of marriage. I was finally free from bondage. Free from tyranny. Free from a grip on my life that I had known as long as I could remember. Chris smiled back at me. He grabbed my hands and held them softly.

I looked into the crowd from the stage and was pleased to be among my friends. Then I saw how dysfunctional my family was. Both of my biological parents were sitting in the pew next to one another. They hadn't seen each other in almost twenty years. I saw a hateful man, sad, worn out, empty. I saw an abuser with nothing left from all he had worked for in his life. He was a lonely pathetic old man with nothing.

When I looked at my Mom, all I saw was the shell of a once beautiful woman, a former prostitute and drug addict. I saw a wife and mother of an abused and hurt person. Yet, we had so much in common. She carried the same pain that I did, the daughter of an abuser. The person I once called Mom, now looked like a medical experiment gone wrong.

I looked at both of my parents knowing that I didn't want to be like either one of them. I also wondered what they would look like sitting there if they had stayed married and were happy. I couldn't help but think of the "what ifs." These two people were stand-ins. They were symbols for parents.

Chris' parents, on the other hand, were fantastic. They had told me that they are not losing a son, but gaining a daughter. I took joy in knowing that I was being accepted into their family.

Wendy stood next to me as my maid of honor. She lined up next to three other close friends with mauve tea-length bridesmaids dresses.

Chris stood next to Randy Scott, our long time friend and youth group leader. Chris and I stood next to each other while Randy spoke.

Randy opened up the service, "I've known these two for a long time. The first time Chris saw Ramie, he asked me who she was and I told him. Then he said 'I'm gonna marry her!'" The audience burst into laughter. I was pleased to have a little levity among such complex family dynamics. Chris beamed, knowing that he was right to make the prediction. He had every reason to be so bold.

I laughed and stared at Chris. That was the first time I ever heard that story.

Randy continued, "And now that prophecy is being lived out."

That day, my name was changed for the second time. This time it was by my choice. I became Ramie Stenzel, and proudly wear that name.

The service was short but the celebration was long.

When we cut the cake together, Chris cut a small slice.

I took the knife from his hand, "No we need it to be bigger." The crowd started laughing, knowing that a cake war was impending. I cut out a piece the size of my hand, making sure it was thick with sugary frosting.

When he had armed himself and stood ready, I attacked first. With the glazed top pointed directly at his face, I shoved it in at him aiming at his nose. After initial contact, I swirled it all around his face and down to his chest. I took a step back and admired my work. Frosting covered his face. His coat, shirt, and tie were glazed with sugar. Pieces of cake sat on his left shoulder.

He immediately reciprocated with a piece pointed at me. He attacked and I closed my eyes. Cake covered my face and it went up my nose, and all over my hair. I laughed hysterically. Little pieces of cake were all over my beautiful dress.

All of our close friends cheered. They expected this type of behavior from us. I reached into the cake and grabbed another piece and threw it at him. He did the same and we had a mini food fight between the two of us. The event probably lasted about five seconds, and everyone in the crowd sent up whoops of joy. The tile floor was slippery with cake. I blew my nose and frosting came out.

We enjoyed a long night with friends and family. My fairy tale wedding was complete.

Chapter 15

I was scared to be a mom. I knew that the baby growing within me was going to be wonderful and beautiful, but I was afraid of being a mom. Anxiety gripped me whenever I imagined stepping into that new role. How could I be a mother when nobody was a mother to me?

Intellectually, I knew I was far from what my own mother was. I was mentally stable. I wasn't strung out on drugs. I was married, had a stable job, and a husband.

This all made for a firm foundation upon which to start a family. Yet emotionally, I was scared. I dreaded having a baby look into my eyes with expectation that I would provide for him. It was up to me to love and care for him in ways that I never experienced myself. I didn't know if I had what it takes.

I declared to myself that our family situation would be different for this baby than it was for me. Nobody would ever lock this baby in the trunk of a car. This baby would never be left alone for hours or days at a time. This baby would not be taken away from me and sent to foster care or to an abusive father.

I sat in a recliner in our small house and felt my growing belly. I looked over at Chris who was watching a ball game on the television. This amazing husband was true to his vows. He grew up with a good mother and father and they were excellent role models for him to follow. I was confident that Chris was never going to harm my baby. He was warm and compassionate. He communicated in a healthy and positive manner. None of the terrible things that happened to me at my father's hand would ever happen to this precious child.

I was at peace that we were stable, healthy, and capable. I simply had a gap in my life where the role mother should have been. Day by day, my thoughts echoed in my mind. Month after month, as the child grew inside me, I grew in confidence that I could be a mother. My love for this child grew to proportions that I had never known before. I decided that I would give him the unconditional love Cheryl gave me. I wanted to have traditions he would remember his whole life. I wanted him to be who God created him to be and not try and change him to fit my expectations or standards. God created him in His image – not mine! Mostly I wanted to be the mom to him that I always wanted someone else to be for me.

Micah Dean Stenzel was born Jan 4, 1994 at Aurora Regional Hospital in Aurora Colorado. We named him after Chris and his Dad, who all had the middle name Dean. I loved watching Chris hold Micah. Joy filled my heart as I witnessed him rock the little tiny baby back and forth with a smile on his face. I knew Chris would be a great dad. Growing up he had a solid role model for fatherhood. His dad was an anchor in his life and Chris knew that he could step into that new role easily.

On the other hand, I had to live up to a role that was foreign to me. I prayed that day and thanked God for this baby boy. I vowed that I would be the mother to him that I always wanted someone to be for me. I had bonded with him in utero but now that he was in my arms I could only pray that I would be the mom he needed me to be and that through my mistakes he would survive and be everything a parent hopes for a child.

Micah was a happy baby, a total cuddle bug. His first word besides "dada" was "fish." As he grew, he loved everything about fish and fishing. He had a Mickey Mouse fishing pole as a toddler and would catch plastic fish out of the fountain at his grandparents' house. Even at that early age his Papa would take him to the pond by their house and catch Blue Gill. He fished everywhere he could find water – even the toilet.

In the fall of 1996 I was pregnant with our second child. Micah was a toddler. He was a joy, and I no longer had the fear of taking the motherly role. I looked forward to having two babies.

One evening while I was doing laundry and watching Micah, the phone rang.

I answered, "Hello?"

"Hey Ramie, it's Dad."

My heart sank. I didn't say anything.

"I called to give you some news."

"Okay."

"I've been feeling exhausted and tired for the last few months so I went to see a doctor. They told me I have stomach cancer."

I didn't know what to say. "You what?"

"I have cancer. I'm being treated in Tijuana. The docs down here seem to be good but the treatment is a long haul."

"I'm glad you're getting good care."

There was a long pause. "I need to tell you about two life insurance policies that I've got. You are the beneficiary."

The conversation had gone from disconcerting to awkward in a few short words.

He said, "Don't worry about my assets. Other than some gold nuggets and some cash hidden under one of the kitchen tiles at the house, I don't have anything of value worth coming for."

After we hung up, I really didn't have any emotion. I had no frame of reference to understand the concept of a man with stomach cancer. No box to put that in. I figured that since he was being treated for his condition, he would be okay. I didn't understand that stomach cancer is often discovered in the later stages of the disease and therefore often advances quickly. I didn't know that treatment for stomach cancer in the 1990s was limited. I had no idea that the trip from Mulegé to Tijuana was over twelve hours by car. I didn't understand how his treatment would be terribly difficult and wipe him out both physically and financially.

Normally, when the house phone rang, it was always a friend or neighbor wanting to get together. My mind routinely steered clear of memories of Dad. There was no longer any connection to him. So in December, when the phone rang again, I answered the phone expecting to hear a cheerful friend but instead heard a weak voice, "Ramie?"

I wasn't sure who it was. I said, "Dad?"

"How are you doing?"

"Fine, how are you?"

120

"I've been struggling. They stopped the cancer treatments."

"Are you getting better?"

"Not really. In fact, it's the other extreme. The medicine was too much for me to handle. Plus the drive back and forth to Tijuana is a killer."

I didn't know what to say. "Those roads are pretty tough."

"They stopped all the cancer treatment. The only medicine I'm on now is morphine."

"How long do you have?"

"Don't worry about that. Let's not talk about that.

"Okay."

"I do have one final request for you."

My eyes grew wide. *He's gonna do it! Oh good, I'm going to get an apology or some sort of acknowledgement for what he had done in the past.*

My heart ached for him to realize the unending pain and suffering that he had caused me. I needed for him to apologize. If he were to reach out with a simple apology, I knew I would accept it immediately! I wanted to love him. I knew our relationship would never be healthy, whole, unified. But if he just apologized, that would start the process of mending the wound. It would seal the gap, the chasm between us. But he stood in the way. I still felt his fists against my head, his feet in my back, abuse. His domineering prideful words of hatred and scorn reverberated in my head.

If only he were to reach out in humility and wisdom and ask for forgiveness. I'd grant it in a heartbeat.

I said, "Okay, what's your request?"

He said, "Don't tell Yvonne or Whitney that I'm dying."

What?

"I don't want Yvonne coming after what little financially I've got left."

Are you kidding me? In this phone call, which might be our last, your final words to your daughter are about your money! Really? That's all you can think about?

I took a deep breath and considered what he was saying. Whitney had disowned him and had not spoken to him in years. Yvonne and I hadn't spoken since she left. For me to not speak to them was easy, it meant to simply continue doing what I was already doing.

I shook my head and a tear formed in my eyes. "Sure."
I honored his request.

. . . . .

Rodney Jan Stenzel was born February 17, 1997. We named
him after my dad and me, we all had the middle name Jan. At 21½
inches long and almost eleven pounds, he was a monster of a baby.
The delivery was hard on me physically and they did major repair
work afterwards. He was so big, the hospital t-shirt didn't even cover
his belly button.

He had blonde hair and big blue eyes. In the process of the
birth the doctor said he had aspirated meconium. This meant that
some nasty junk got into his lungs. They moved him to the neonatal
intensive care unit (NICU) where they sunk a tube into his lungs and
sucked it out. He was fine after that but we stayed a couple of days in
the hospital due to the repair after the delivery.

The day after Rodney was born, we had plenty of visitors and
the phone in the hospital room was constantly ringing. At one point
Chris handed me the phone and said, "It's my sister Kathie." She was
watching Micah back at our house.

I said, "Hi Kath, how's Micah?"

"He's doing great. I can't wait 'til you bring home his little
brother."

"Not so little!"

She said, "Ramie, congratulations on Rodney. I hear he's
huge!"

I laughed, "They don't make them any bigger!"

She was quiet for a moment then said, "I've got something to
tell you."

I said, "Okay, what's up?"

She paused then said, "I hate to be the one to tell you this, but
I got a call from your Dad's friend in Mexico."

The smile ran away from my face. I choked up and said, "He's
gone isn't he?"

She was quiet for a moment, then said, "Yes, he passed
yesterday."

I said, "Thanks for letting me know." I handed the phone to Chris who hung up. I started crying.

Chris looked at me and said, "He's gone?"

I said, "Yes he's gone."

I wasn't crying because he was dead. I cried because I would never hear him say he was sorry. Maybe he wasn't sorry. Maybe he never perceived what he did to me was wrong.

I can't even begin to describe the emotions of that day.

My mind drifted to a snapshot of the last time I saw him. At the airport in Mexico, the fabric of his shirt held up so that I could see his gun. His parting display was not a hug, a kiss on the cheek, or even a tender pat on the back. Rather his final good-bye was a death threat. The last gesture he gave me on that trip was the same as when he made me drink poison.

I hated him.

I remembered all of the things he had done to me. It was so obvious that it was wrong. Nobody should perform that kind of abuse. There were laws against it. He should have been arrested and thrown in prison for what he did. He killed Pandy, murdered Grandma. He paid to have me raped, twice. He was terrible, a terrible father, a terrible human being. He knew he was wrong but never acknowledged it. He never apologized, and now he never would.

I had imagined conversations with him where he reaches out and apologizes for everything. I longed to hear him say that he was sorry. I had hoped for reconciliation with him. Now all that hope was officially shattered.

I never heard Dad say he loved me or that he was proud of me. I never would hear those words. Ever. He was gone. There was no chance of reconciliation. No hope for any type of meaningful relationship.

I lay in the hospital bed, dumbfounded. Chris told my doctor and the nurses what was going on. They graciously added two days to my hospital stay. The doctor and the nurses at the hospital were fantastic.

I lay alone with my thoughts. I could not wrap my head around the emotions of the day. I felt every sentiment possible. When my thoughts drifted to Dad I felt a pit in my stomach. The hair on the back of my neck rose. I felt fear. I was livid, furious, frustrated, exasperated, and disgusted. I remembered his cruelty and contempt for life. My heart harbored hatred, pain, and remorse. At the thought of his loss I somehow felt sadness and grief. Then in response to my own compassion, I felt surprise and even shame.

Then as I pondered the new baby boy struggling for his life in the NICU my heart cried out for him. I had only held him for a few moments before they had to take him away. I felt devotion and joy. I had great expectations for him. Yet, he was still in the hospital. I felt fear, worry, and utter dread. I was baffled, anxious, helpless and impatient. I was in despair. I wanted to hold my baby.

When Chris came into the room holding Micah, a nurse wheeled Rodney into the room. Thankfully, he no longer needed the critical care at the NICU. Suddenly, my heart leapt for joy. I felt compassion, sympathy. Chris said that Rodney was going to be fine in a few days. I felt optimism. I was thankful to our kind and loving God. My heart poured out with love and was filled with joy. With Chris by my side, I had courage. I knew that when we brought Rodney home we would be okay. I had a moment of modesty, humility, and patience.

Then, when I closed my eyes, my father re-appeared. Though he was gone, he was still present with me. The fear and anger returned. Startled, I opened my eyes. Thankfully, Chris was there. I didn't want to close my eyes again. The day seemed to go on forever. I was exhausted.

There was a knock on the door and Yvonne's face appeared around the corner. "Can I come in to visit?"

I was shocked. I had not seen or talked to her much since the divorce. She explained, "I work in the cardiology floor in this hospital, two floors up. I happened to see your name on the patient list. The nurses are always talking about the babies that are born in here. I heard about the biggest baby ever and that it was yours. Then I heard about Kenny."

She stopped her story at that point. I had nothing to add. The silence was incredibly awkward.

We made small talk about my baby and she was happy to hear that he was out of the NICU. Then she said, "How did Kenny die?"

"Stomach cancer."

"How long did you know?"

"He called me in November."

"That's four months ago. Why didn't you tell me?"

"He asked me not to. He was very specific and asked me not to tell you or Whitney."

She was visibly upset.

I was under no obligation to tell her. They were divorced. I remained quiet.

Yvonne asked, "What is going to happen to Grandma's pink depression wear?"

"I've got the china set. Dad gave it to me when he moved to Mexico. He made it clear that he wanted me to have that."

She was disgusted. It was obvious that she wanted to get her hands on it. It was mine, and she wasn't going to get it. She had come to visit, not to console me or connect with me in any way, but simply because she wanted the china set. Another series of emotions rolled in as I was disappointed, sad, and angry.

After a little more small talk, she excused herself.

The china set meant the world to me. It is my only family heirloom and my solitary connection to my wonderful Grandma. Dad wanted me to have it. If I could choose an object to remember Dad, it would have been one of Dad's pipes. For some reason, his pipe was nostalgic. Only positive smell memories come from his Nighthawk flavor tobacco.

Later that day, Whitney called the phone in the hospital room. She was upset that I didn't tell her Dad was dying. She lamented the fact that she was denied the chance to make amends with him. I was shocked.

Really? She disowned him years ago. She even took Sherman's last name until she was married. Over the next few weeks, we spoke on and off. The conversations were long enough for her to find out if her name was on any of the insurance policies. Once she found out that she was cut off she stopped talking to me.

After a few days, I was discharged from the hospital. Chris was a huge help at home during the first week. He cleaned the kitchen, did the laundry and helped with everything around the house.

I closed my eyes to rest. As I slumbered, I had a dream in which I was transported back to Mexico. I was heading to see where Dad was buried. In my mind's eye, I saw a rectangular opening in the brown desert earth. A staircase led to an underground tunnel. I stepped on the first of the stairs and felt a cool breeze. I descended one step at a time until I was completely underground. I found myself in a type of mausoleum with a glass window separating me from a casket on a wooden table. Inside the casket was the body of my father. It was lit up on the inside and I could see him clearly. He lay there wearing a suit and tie. His hands were crossed over his chest like they are traditionally positioned at a wake or funeral.

I stood there looking at him through the glass. Then, all of a suddenly, he turned his head and looked directly at me. His eyes were deep red, crimson like blood. His dead face was staring at me with evil eyes.

Panicked, I turned on my heel and ran up and out of there as fast as I could. Crying, I was desperate to get away.

I opened my eyes and realized that I was at home in the safety of my bedroom. It had been a dream. A nightmare. My heart was racing and beads of sweat covered my forehead. The sheets were soaked in sweat. I sat up. It took me a while to put the pieces together and sort through what was real and what was a dream.

A couple days after we came home from the hospital, the phone rang.

I answered, "Hello?"

"Hola Señora Ramie. This is Fernando, a friend of your father's, in Mulegé."

What could he possibly want?

"Yes, hello Fernando."

He asked, "Are you coming to get your father's possessions?"

"I'm sorry, I just had a baby and had major repair work done and could not get released to travel."

"Congratulations on your new baby Señora! I'm sure Señor Kenny would be proud to know he is an abuelo."

I said nothing.

He laughed and continued, "I do need to tell you that we buried him the day after he died."

I didn't ask where. I imagine they rolled him up in his bed covers, tossed him in the back of a pick-up truck and buried him wherever they felt like it – just like they did with Grandma.

I simply said, "Thank you."

He added, "It's also customary in Mexico that if the family doesn't come to collect the deceased person's possessions within 48 hours, we open the house to the town."

"What does that mean?"

126

"They come and take whatever they want."

I had no response.

"Señora, it's already past the 48 hour mark and my amigos cannot hold off any longer."

"Let the town take what they want."

"Gracias Señora. Adios."

No apology. No funeral. No closure.

A week after Rodney was born Chris came home from work and informed me that he had lost his job. The added stress was nothing new. Together we started searching for new employment opportunities for him right away.

Then, when Rodney was a tender three weeks old, he woke me up in the middle of the night coughing. I fed him and changed him, but he wouldn't go back to sleep. He was coughing constantly and having a hard time getting his breath. I knew the difference between a fussy baby and a baby who was in trouble. This was the latter.

I woke Chris up and told him what was going on. He packed Micah and Rodney into the car and we headed back to the hospital. They diagnosed him with respiratory syncytial virus (RSV) and he spent a week back in the NICU.

In just three weeks we had endured a birth, a death, the loss of a job, and a child in the hospital with a major illness. There are plenty of psychological studies out there that talk about major stressors that we go through in life. We seemed to stack them up.

I called Margaret and the Callahans to talk a little. They listened, but I didn't have the energy to talk about Dad with them. I was overwhelmed. With a sore body, sick baby, a jobless husband, I didn't have the capacity to deal with Dad's passing. The emotional rollercoaster I endured in the hospital needed to end.

The friends who came and helped around the house gave their condolences but they didn't know Dad. They didn't know my history, or the pain he had caused. They had no way of knowing what his passing meant to me. If I had tried to discuss it with them, I'd have to bring up the past with him to be able to explain my emotions. I resorted to my tried and true method of dealing with problems. I stuffed it deep down inside.

Chapter 16

About six months after my dad died, I received a box on my doorstep. It was a large cardboard box with dented corners and water damage indicating it had been through a fair amount of trauma during its travel. As I opened the door to retrieve it, I curiously looked at the postmark. It was from Mexico. My thoughts ran back to Dad. I hadn't requested anything from his estate. In fact, I was pretty clear telling Dad's friend Fernando that I didn't want anything at all.

What could this be? Why would any of his friends do this?

It was clearly addressed to me, my name scrawled on the package as the addressee. I brought the box inside and set it on my kitchen table. Without any fanfare, I grabbed a knife and cut through the tape and lifted the cardboard flaps. Inside was an assortment of my dad's things. I started to rummage through the items pulling them out one by one. It was not packed with any sort of care. There was no bubble wrap, no newspaper around any of the items, no cover letter discussing what the package was or whom it was for. It was all just thrown in together.

I took out a stack of papers at the top of the box. The first one was a certificate proclaiming Kenny Smith to be "Salesman of the year" for 3M National Outdoor Advertising. It was ordained with the company's logo and signed by the CEO. The next page was similar, another award indicating success in the office. The stack was significant, almost a half inch thick. Most of them were water soaked and torn. The many accolades that once hung proudly on his wall were now nothing more than trash. I placed them on the table and looked back in the box.

I saw my dad's Bible. It was the one I had bought for him. It was still beautiful and smelled like new leather. The pages were stuck together and the spine was perfectly stiff. It didn't take a CSI forensic scientist to determine that nobody had ever read through the precious pages of this wonderful book.

I sat the Bible down and started to pull out my dad's car racing trophies. I chuckled. I pulled them out and saw that they were no longer shiny and perfect; rather, they were dusty and broken. I remembered being punished for failing to dust them properly. I was accused of lying. I was scolded, ridiculed, and beaten because of these things. As I pulled them out of the box, I didn't clean them or even consider wiping the grime from the surface. I simply set them on the table next to the other relics. The once treasured wood and brass objects were now broken and meaningless. They were all that remained of my dad – a raggedy collection of tarnished idols.

The rest of the contents were a few personal papers that meant nothing at all to me, and my dad's wallet. The only thing in his wallet was his driver's license and some business cards. I placed all the items back in the box and gave it a little shove to the middle of the table. It didn't make me upset, nostalgic, or anything at all. In my mind, the only thing that the box did for me was to confirm that my dad was really dead.

With the box as an unwelcomed centerpiece on my kitchen table, my thoughts drifted back to my past. I began to think about my dad for a while, then my memories drifted to my mom who was no longer in my life. I had no parents. In retrospect, looking back on my life, you could say that I never did. However, I did have an older brother and sister that I hadn't seen or heard from since we were little. I remembered that day, twenty years earlier in the in the courtroom, the last time I saw David and Lisa. That was the day that we were painfully separated. I remember sitting with Elise while my brother sat with his grandparents and my sister with her foster parents on the day our family was officially torn apart. I wondered what had happened in their lives and pondered the thought of trying to find each of them.

I remembered David sitting with his grandparents in the courtroom. Surely he had lived with them until he finished high school. *They should be easier to track down.* I started there. I picked up the phone and dialed the number for information and asked the operator if she had the number for Don and Dee Maggard in Scottsdale, Arizona. I heard the rattle of the keyboard as she pulled up the number. She and rattled it off to me and I scribbled the number down and immediately dialed it.

I talked to David's grandma and she was excited to speak with me. I asked if she knew where David was and she immediately gave me his number. I thanked her and wished her well. My heart was jumping with excitement. My memories with my siblings were limited and almost all negative. I was hoping to establish some good ones. I wasn't sure if David would talk to me or even wanted to be found but I gave it a shot. It took me a couple of tries to actually get in touch with him. Once we connected, we were both excited to catch up. I filled him in on my life and he told me about his. He was living in Arizona, an avid biker who worked in a bike shop selling and fixing bicycles. He had never gotten married, and had no kids. He said, the name David reminded him too much of his childhood so he changed his name to Dane.

We discussed our mother. He said he had been in contact with her but had not seen her. He was angry with her and wanted her to own up to what she had done to us as kids. She never took responsibility for what she did and my brother could never get over that.

I invited him to come up to visit and he bought a ticket to come visit me. It was a tearful reunion. We had a lot of catching up to do. Since he was a few years older than I was, he remembered more than I did about our childhood. Clearly, his pain and rejection were deeper than mine. Our time was enjoyable together and after a pleasant weekend, he told me about his life and how he had lived in various places over the years. I could see that he was happy riding his bike and living the life of a nomad.

In one of our conversations, I asked about our sister Lisa. He told me that she was living in Florida. I jotted down her number before he left. We parted on good terms but communication was limited after that.

This was so easy! How did I find them both with hardly any searching?

130

I was excited to contact Lisa. She was the oldest so she would remember the most. I was hoping she would have some good memories of me as a child and us together. One day while the boys were napping, I called Lisa. The phone rang quite a few times before she answered.

"Hello?"

I said, "Hey, this is Sara – well my name is Ramie now…"

She interrupted, "I know, David said you would be calling." There was a hesitation in her voice as if she wasn't sure she wanted to talk with me.

We made small talk and I filled her in on Chris and the boys and where we were living. She explained that she was living with her boyfriend in Florida. She had lived with her foster mom until she passed away. She was old enough to be on her own at that point. Lisa never married or had any kids. After a short conversation, I said, "I'd like to call again, would that be okay?"

She agreed and we hung up. We talked on and off for a few weeks, each of our conversations were short. One day I asked her if we could get together so we could see one another. Again she hesitated, but agreed only if I came to Florida. I agreed and she offered to buy my ticket.

I made the arrangements, and Chris was happy to take care of the boys while I was gone. I sat in the plane wondering if I would recognize Lisa when I saw her. When I deplaned, she was there to greet me. I knew exactly who she was – tall, sandy blonde hair, and dressed to impress. She looked like a model out of a magazine. I was teary and excited to see her but I got the feeling she wasn't as excited as I was. Her hug was quick and almost mechanical, not your typical reunion.

We exchanged a few greetings and headed out of the airport. As we pulled up to the house, I laid eyes on her huge home surrounded by palm trees. The inside was gorgeous, I felt like I was back in Kenny's house as a kid and didn't want to touch anything.

Lisa introduced me to her boyfriend, Donald. He was gorgeous, straight out of GQ magazine and was obviously very wealthy. Lisa didn't work; she said her job was taking care of Donald. We spent the weekend together shopping and going to the beach. It felt like Lisa was more of my tour guide and while I peppered her with questions about where she lived, she gave basic answers. Strangely, she seemed to be making no effort to get to know me. I tried to ask her questions about our life together as kids but she would either change the subject fast or would walk away as if she never heard me. Her walls were noticeably up and weren't coming down any time soon.

I was puzzled. *Was she that hurt? Or maybe it was me? Was she disappointed in me? Was I not what she dreamed I would be?*

After the weekend was over, she took me back to the airport and I boarded the plane with these questions reverberating in my mind. I was teary, but had no tears of pain or sorrow. I was simply sad. I came home more confused than when I left.

I felt empty.

It was obvious that we weren't going to be close and I didn't even get one comment from her about myself as a baby or any of my questions answered. I called Lisa when I got home and thanked her again for a fun weekend.

She said, "Sara, or Ramie – whoever you are – I have a happy life and you don't fit in it."

I furrowed my brow. I said, "Okay."

She continued, "You are a part of a painful past. I was forced to take care of you. Without me you would have died, you and David both. You even started calling me 'mommy' at the end. I was only twelve!"

I was shocked.

She wasn't done. "I'm sorry, but seeing you this past weekend only reminded me of Jane and the pain she caused us."

Her voice was emotionless. Her tone wasn't elevated. Her cadence was steady.

She said, "I'm sorry but I can't have any further contact with you. Please don't reach out to me ever again. Forget I even exist." I wanted to thank her for all that she did for me, but before I had the chance, she hung up the phone.

I never heard from her again and I respected her wishes to be left alone.

Her rejection ached in my heart. I had missed my chance. I spent a weekend with her and never thanked her for everything she had done. I didn't realize it until the phone call. But after she opened my eyes, I could see it through her perspective. She had it worse than David or I did. She put up with far more than either of us. She took on the role of mother as a twelve year old! I didn't know I called her mommy!

I stood there with the phone in my hand. The tone changed and I knew I had to hang it up. I wanted to talk with her again. I wanted to be able to express appreciation for keeping me fed, changed, clothed, and protected. She consoled me the best she could but she never let me get that conversation out.

David and Lisa both remember more than I did and certainly suffered more. It's to Lisa's credit that we were a pack and we stuck together to survive. I will always be forever thankful for them and what they did for me.

Chapter 17

Chris found a new job and we settled into the life of a family of four. We managed to purchase a small house and both worked. I longed to stay home more with the boys and it didn't take long to discover that Denver was too expensive for us. If I was to stay home to raise the boys we needed to live somewhere more affordable. But where would we go?

As we dreamed of where we wanted to move I mentioned a little town called Burley Idaho. I had a friend that lived there, I had visited her before and loved the area. As we tossed ideas around, Chris reminisced about his time in the Navy. He loved the time he spent up in Whidbey Island Naval Base. He told me about the beautiful waterfront, the parks and a thousand things to do in the Pacific Northwest. He had a lot of great memories from his time there and knew that the housing market was more affordable than the Denver region. He also had some close family friends that lived there.

Together, we decided to think and dream about it. However, the house we owned anchored us. In a stagnant housing market, we worried about being unable to sell. We did not want to move unless we sold it without taking a loss. We decided to put our house on the market and pray. We felt that if it sold quickly, we knew we were supposed to move.

Our home sold within twenty-four hours of being on the market to the first person who looked at it. Our prayer was answered as plain as day. Over the next thirty days we packed up the house. Moving day came with a U-Haul and car packed, two kids, a dog, and a turtle.

Chris' parents came to see us off. They helped pack. With motherly concern, Chris' mom asked, "Where are you headed?"

He said, "Towards Washington."

She raised her eyebrows. "Towards Washington? That's not really a destination. It's more of a direction."

Chris laughed it off, "Don't worry Mom. We'll be fine."

With a compass setting as our guide we headed off. We had no home to go to and no job. As the wheels rolled, we were leaving on faith. Chris drove the U-Haul and I followed in our sedan. We drove northwest up through Wyoming and into the southern edge of Idaho. After traveling all day long, with multiple stops for the boys, we rolled into Burley to see my friends for dinner. They welcomed us with open arms. We enjoyed a meal and afterwards relaxed in their living room. When they heard our non-descript plans, they suggested that we stay in town with them. We enjoyed their company and lightheartedly agreed. After a while they asked, "If we get Chris a job at the local chemical plant, would you two stay?"

We agreed. The following morning, Chris filled out an application, they granted him an interview and was offered the job the following afternoon. With a new job and friends in town, we settled into our new life in Idaho. We rented a house then a year later, we moved into our own home. It was a lovely three bedroom, two bathroom 1800 square foot house. Sitting on almost an acre of land. There was plenty of room for the boys to run and make lots of memories.

We celebrated our new home with the birth of our third son Tyler Joe. He was perfect and completed our family of five. He was my smallest baby weighing in at almost 8 pounds. Though large by any normal baby measurement, he was puny compared to his brothers – the runt of the litter. He acquired the nickname "Pune" from day one.

We loved raising the boys in a small town. We joined a church and met a lot of friends and bonded with a small group we called our family. We raised our kids together, went to church together and did life together. Praise Chapel was an older church with a congregation of about 200. Young couples and lots of kids. The boys were always involved in church activities, school and 4-H.

When Tyler was six months old, I struggled to lift him in and out of his crib because of severe lower back pain. I was no stranger to pain, having dealt with all kinds of pain through my life, so I put up with it for a long time. When I couldn't put Tyler in his crib or lift him out anymore, I realized that this was serious. The searing pain gripped me and forced me flat on my back with my legs on a chair. I finally found a position that gave me relief. Whenever I moved I suffered the consequences.

I made an appointment with a Chiropractor. He examined me and did some manipulation of my back and spine. I left feeling better. When I returned home, I saw piles of laundry, a kitchen that needed to be cleaned and children that needed care. My motherly instinct drew me to get everything done around the house that had to be done. Within a day, the pain returned with a vengeance.

I made an appointment with our family practice physician. He examined me and sent me to a physical therapist. She told me to do some exercises and stretching. I went home and did everything she recommended, but got no relief.

I called the doctor and told him that the physical therapy was a failure. He sent me to another doctor who performed several cortisone shots in my back. Then they performed a laser procedure on my back. Nothing helped. The doctor was frustrated but not surprised. He sent me to a neurologist in Salt Lake City.

Though the pain never left, the doctor bills were getting out of control. Every visit was another couple of hundred dollars. I got familiar with terms like co-payment, deductable, and the dreaded explanation of benefits (EOB). I looked at the pile of bills on our kitchen table. I had been through all of this and still had no relief from the pain. *What were we doing? Could we keep gong on like this? Maybe we should call it quits.*

I held the referral slip to the Neurologist in my hand and told Chris, "This is getting out of hand. Maybe I shouldn't go."

Chris said, "Let's give the specialist a try. You never know, maybe he'll see something the other guys didn't see?"

I called the number on the slip and made an appointment. We drove three hours to a hospital in Salt Lake City. The drive was physically torturous since I couldn't sit for any period of time. My back felt like a dagger was twisting in my flesh. When we got there, the process started all over again at the new office with paperwork, insurance documentation, and a litany of questions. Dr. Mark Reichman entered the room with my chart in his hands. He had short, dark hair, and a white lab coat. He was professional in his manner, caring but without levity or humor. I told him about the pain I was having, in my back, and how it was shooting down my legs. I told him about the Chiropractor, Physical Therapist, and the injections.

He heard my story and concluded for me, "None of it helped, right?"

I was surprised, "How did you know that?"

He said flatly, "If it had helped, you wouldn't be here."

I did my best to smile.

He said, "Listen, you haven't surprised me at all. People have lots of back pain, and we have a number of ways to help. When back pain is so bad that people have leg pain, that is how I know it's serious. I'd like to start by getting a little more information."

He took a few minutes and looked me over. He had me stand, extend my arms, and move this way and that. Finally after a series of slow calisthenics, he let me sit down again. He asked about my pregnancies, the size of each baby – lots of details. Then he said, "Listen, I don't know what we're going to find, but something significant is going on to cause all this pain. Let's start some X-rays and go from there."

He filled out a little paperwork and handed it to his nurse. She took me to an X-ray department where I got several plain film x-rays of my back. Then it was off to another room for an MRI. He reviewed the results and then sent me back to get a full body x-ray.

Once again, I sat on the cold exam table waiting for the doctor. When he returned, he had a solemn expression on his face. He sat down next to me and with his clipboard on his lap he asked, "Have you ever been in a car accident?"

I said, "No."

He furrowed his brow and scratched his chin. Then he asked, "Have you heard been kicked by large animal?"

"No. Why are you asking me these questions?"

He paused, looked over the X-rays again and asked, "Have you ever fallen from high place? Like off a ladder or out of a tree?"

"No."

He put his clipboard on the countertop and looked at me. With the sigh he said, "My god girl, what happened to you?"

Tears welled up in my eyes. I looked around the room. The tile walls matched the tile floor. This clinic had the same look and feel as all the other clinics I had been in. Dad had instilled the proper decorum of lying and storytelling to get through. The nurse's words reverberated in my head, "We don't feel sorry for people like you!"

But this time was different. I hadn't done anything wrong. Dad wasn't there. Nobody was threatening me a gun. I wasn't suicidal. There wasn't a nurse looming over me with derogatory words. I wasn't ordered to keep quiet.

I looked at the doctor and thought, *After all these years someone was asking me what happened.*

I felt terrified and relieved at the same time.

I have freedom to start talking about my father.

I looked at the doctor's graying temples and knew that nothing I said could be used against me. I felt the blood drain from my face. "My father was pretty hard on me."

He waited for me to elaborate.

I looked him in the eye, "Really hard."

He understood that I was talking about physical abuse. "Take a look at the X-rays with me." He showed me plain film x-rays and we look at them together. The bones of my wrists had both been broken, multiple times.

He said, "With this kind of injury, we like to set the bones so they will heal. Yours were never set."

I stayed quiet.

He continued to point out my ribs. "There are several broken ribs both in the front and back."

I felt my ribs, and remembered his kicks after I was on the ground. I remembered being kicked down the stairs.

"Let's take a look at the films of your brain." He spoke clinically, without humor or condescension. "The MRI shows that your brain has scar tissue build up that we only see with multiple concussions. Did you have head trauma?"

I remembered being thrown against a wall. "Yes, a number of times."

He paused. "I know this is a lot to take in. You really came in here for me to look at your back. Why don't we do that?"

I said, "Sure. I can't imagine that there is any good news there."

He sighed, "Not really. There's a lot of damage in the lumbar vertebrae."

I saw the images. He showed me an example of what a normal MRI of a back looks then showed my mine again. In comparison it looked like a train wreck.

My injured body was laid bare. He saw through me and I had told the truth. I was terrified, yet relieved. A heavy burden I no longer had to carry. I couldn't argue with or deny what the X-rays clearly showed. I didn't have to lie. I could speak freely. I was angry. Under my breath I called my dad every cuss word I could think of.

Even though he's dead he's still controlling of my life.

My words were few but admitting that I had been hurt at the hands of my father was a start to healing and freedom.

I asked the doc, "Why after all these years am I having so many back issues?"

He took a deep breath and replied, "A body can only take so much. Certainly, our bodies start breaking down as we get older. When you left your Dad's house, there was a lot of damage done. Add on top of that three very large babies and traumatic births. That was more than your lower back could handle and it started to break down."

He told me about other things including a surgery to fix the damage. Honestly, I don't remember a single thing he said. He talked for a while, but my mind was in the past. Scenario after scenario started running rampant through my mind. I remembered Dad's hands on my wrists. I remembered his foot sinking deep into my back over and over again.

The nurse helped me set up a surgery date and I left the office. The long drive home was more than I could bear. Every mile reminded me of the source of my pain. Dad. Not only did I feel damage emotionally and physically, like I had for the past two decades, but now looking at the films and hearing what the doctor said, I was able to see my personal brokenness from the inside.

A few weeks later, Dr. Reichman performed a laminectomy to repair the disks in my back that had blown. When I went home the next day, I was in more pain than before. The surgical pain added to the pain I always suffered with. After a few weeks, the surgical pain had eased, but the old pain never did. Two years later Chris and I were back in the doctor Reichman's office talking about another surgery.

This time we pretty much knew what to expect. I dreaded every moment. In the doctor's office, I waited on the cold exam table wearing nothing but the flimsy hospital gown designed to combine humility with humiliation. Chris understood my angst and saw a small doll sized skeleton standing on the countertop. He reached into my purse and pulled out two blue breath mints and placed them in the eye sockets of the skeleton. Then he proceeded to roll up a piece of paper from a surgical instruction pamphlet and put it in the edge of the mouth. He then interlocked the hands in front of the skeleton pelvic area. The little skeleton was smoking a cigarette, wide eyed and embarrassed because he was naked.

I was annoyed, amused, then I finally laughed. But when the doctor came in with a clipboard full of important paperwork, he looked at Chris' handiwork and wasn't amused.

He said, "Since the repair didn't work the best way to move forward is to do a multilevel spine fusion of the lower back."

My eyes glazed over.

He continued, "We repair the damaged spine and fuse together the vertebrae that are weakened or fractured. We add bone where she needs it and support it all with plates and screws."

Chris' eyes were wide.

I sighed and said, "Will it work?"

He said, "It should work. This is the best chance we have of success for you."

He turned to Chris and said, "The surgery is not without risk. A lot of damage has been done. The spine needs a lot of repair work. I can't guarantee that she will ever walk again but I'll do my best."

Chris reached over and grabbed my hand.

The doctor cautioned, "I don't want to underestimate the risk. There is a chance that you won't be able to do a lot of things after we are done. I can't guarantee the results. I can put the parts in place, do the surgery correctly, but in the end we are depending on your body to heal. Your body might not heal the way we want it to. You may not be able to feel your legs afterwards. You may not be able to walk."

140

Chris and I looked at one another. This is not what we wanted to hear.

He concluded, "But, if everything heals well, you'll be out of pain and return to caring for your kids."

We agreed to the procedure and knew that this was the right thing to do. We filled out the paperwork, made the appointment and went home. When the day came for surgery, I dreaded every moment. Chris was my constant companion and personal comedian. He saw me off as I wheeled into the surgical theater and was there when I woke up.

He asked, "How do you feel?"

In the blur and post-anesthesia confusion, I felt sore and nauseated. I said, "I can feel my feet."

Chris said, "Great news. The incision is from your butt crack all the way up to where your bra is."

I said, "I'm cut from crack to strap."

He laughed, "Yep."

"I just hope this surgery works. I don't know if I could go through any more."

After a few days, I was discharged from the hospital and happy to be home with the boys. One evening, when I got up from the couch, Micah saw the scar on my back. He said, "Mom, you have the longest butt crack in Idaho."

If laughter is the best medicine, the whole family took a good dose that day.

I was flat on my back for three months while the grafted cadaver bone integrated into my spine. I could be up and was encouraged to work but could not bend at all or lift. I had a claw I used to pick things up off the floor and to retrieve clothes from the wash to put in the dryer then from the dryer to fold. The boys were a great help. But being down for three months was a very helpless feeling. Friends brought us meals, shopped for groceries, and came over to clean bathrooms, dust, and vacuum.

When Chris was at work and the boys were at school, I just laid in bed. I had a lot of time to think and pray. I felt like I was being punished with a constant daily reminder of Dad. I remembered every punch and kick. I recalled every blow. The more I thought about it, the angrier I became.

Why, after all these years, do I have to suffer the repercussions of what Dad did to me?

I was angry at God.

I hated my Dad.

I hated God for not protecting me from him.

Wallowing in self-pity, my physical healing progressed. I finally realized I did not want to live this way. I did some serious soul-searching and praying. One thing I knew for sure, I could never forgive Dad.

Chapter 18

I was raised in church. Ever since I was a little girl, three times a week, we put our best clothes on and rode in the car together and sat together in pews. We heard the sermons and sang the songs. I learned every Sunday School children's song, and most of the grown up songs as well. I knew half the hymnal by heart. I went to church camp every summer and I learned to play the part of what a perfect Christian should look like.

At one point, I was even enrolled in a private Christian school called Christian Way. We had Bible teaching every day and chapel was every Wednesday morning. Mrs. Freitag ruled over our classroom of thirty kids. She was a wonderful lady who invested a lot of time into each of us. Every day after lunch, she read from C.S. Lewis' book *The Lion The Witch and The Wardrobe*. Through this allegorical story, I learned the gospel message: Jesus came to the world to save sinners. Mrs. Freitag told us that everybody has sinned, we all have fallen short of God's perfect glory and we all need a savior. Then she explained how because we are sinners, and God is perfect, there is a mighty gulf between us and God. We don't deserve to be with Him, in fact, what we deserve is death.

This was a pretty deep explanation for young kids, but she kept going. She explained that Jesus came into the world and lived a perfect life: He never sinned. Jesus never stole anything, never lied, or did anything that God didn't like. He was perfect. Then when Jesus was crucified on the cross, His death was a substitute for us. He died for us. The *Lion The Witch and The Wardrobe* provided enough of the backdrop that she was able to fill in the rest. I went home and pondered what she taught.

Later on, I accepted the Lord into my heart. During a Sunday School session at Holly Park Chapel the other kids and I sat around a table with our teacher, Ms. Brenda. She gave a short, clear presentation of the gospel. She told the same story that Mrs. Freitag did and concluded with the question, "Does anyone in the class want to accept Jesus into their heart?"

I raised my hand.

Ms. Brenda came over and squatted down next to me and took my hands. She smiled at me and said, "Just repeat after me." She looked at the rest of the kids and said, "Everybody close your eyes and repeat after me."

It was a nice touch to avoid singling out one person and making it awkward. We all nodded and repeated each phrase as she said them.

Phrase by phrase, she said and we repeated, "Dear Lord Jesus, I know that I am a sinner, and I ask for your forgiveness. I believe you died for my sins and rose from the dead. I turn from my sins and invite you to come into my heart and life. I want to trust and follow you as my Lord."

I didn't feel anything. Nothing in my body felt different. But when I opened my eyes and looked around, everyone started clapping like we had just scored a touchdown. I smiled. I figured what I did was right.

Our teacher explained, "The Bible says 'if you confess with your mouth the Lord Jesus and believe in your heart that God has raised Him from the dead, you will be saved.' That's Romans chapter ten verse nine." She squeezed my hand, "You're a Christian, now."

I'm in the club

As I got older, I continued to go to church. I chose to go. At that point it was the norm and it was habit. I went more for the social aspect as a teen and young adult, but seeds were still being sown into my life. I started to realize there were differences in what I was taught as a kid and what I was learning now. I was grabbing at whatever I felt I could do to be at peace at calling myself a Christian but something was still missing.

. . . . .

Raising three boys kept me busy. When Tyler, my youngest, went to Kindergarten I took a job as a vet tech and needed to find a few hours of daycare for him each day. I enrolled him in Kid's First Daycare at the church we attended.

As I was getting the lay of the land at the daycare, I spent time with Jan, the daycare director. She's about fifteen years older than me. As a petite gal, she is tiny but mighty, with a huge heart. She was very classy and quite rigid in her ways. We hit it off right away. Once I had my routine of dropping off Tyler, I made a point to spend a few minutes with Jan. Later, Jan and I began meeting for coffee and soon we became good friends. We frequented Alice's Coffee Shop where we found a secluded spot in the back corner. The coffee shop was also a used bookstore and we had our perfect comfortable place. Surrounded by books, we talked about God, the Bible, and what He was doing in our lives. We shared life together. After we got close, she saw my heart for kids and I had shared a few stories from my past with her. She knew I loved the Lord, and she was becoming a mentor for me. I found that she was fulfilling a Biblical mandate:

Likewise, teach the older women to be reverent in the way they live, not to be slanderers or addicted to much wine, but to teach what is good. Then they can urge the younger women to love their husbands and children, to be self-controlled and pure, to be busy at home, to be kind, and to be subject to their husbands, so that no one will malign the word of God. (Titus 2:3-5)

At Jan's suggestion, I started journaling. I wrote down things that bothered me and things I was struggling with. I processed my triumphs and joys on paper, and when we got together, I looked forward to sharing what I wrote with her.

Jan had a full-time manager at the daycare who managed the day-to-day interaction with the kids, parents, and staff. Jan let her run it and she would pop in now and then to check in. When her manager submitted her resignation, Jan was hunting for a replacement. She needed someone who knew the Lord and was active in church, someone she could trust to run things and who loved those kids. Sitting in Alice's Coffee Shop, she cradled her thick porcelain mug and said, "How would you like to be my new daycare manager?"

I was surprised, "Who? Me?"

She said, "You're the perfect person. You love Jesus, have a heart for the kids, and most importantly, I trust you."

I smiled from ear to ear. "I'd be happy to be your new manager."

Over the next few weeks, I tendered my resignation at the vet clinic and began training under the retiring manager. She showed me the business' routines. I got familiar with the billing process and how to manage the books. I got to know our six employees, all forty kids and their parents. After a couple of months, I ran it on my own.

Most of the kids came from divorced homes. Many of the parents were in jail and grandparents or foster parents were raising the kids. A few of them started life as meth babies.

I connected with these kids! I crocheted a blanket for each one of them. As my hands worked the needle and yarn, each stitch was the word of a prayer for each child. As I covered them up at naptime, I prayed those words over their little lives one at a time.

Many of these kids had some variety of detachment disorder. They were creative in their ways to get attention and they all needed lots of love. I knew how they felt and I had a great love and compassion for them.

One of our regular kids was a four-year-old boy who I'll call Richard. He lived with his mom and rarely saw his Dad. He loved seeing his dad and when he had the opportunity, it was a big deal to him. One Monday morning his mom dropped him off and Richard came in crying. His mom informed us that he had been at his Dad's place through the weekend and had just come home that morning. Our staff got him settled and thanked his mom for the information. It didn't take long for Richard to hit one of the other kids. The staff member put him in a timeout.

When he was released from his timeout, only a few minutes went by before his fists were flying again. He promptly got another time out, then another. The whole morning was full of his misbehavior. The staff members were being stern with him and doling out discipline, but they were getting frustrated.

I heard them say to each other, "What's going on with Richard? He's just been with his dad all weekend. Why isn't he happy?"

While they didn't understand what was going on in his mind, it seemed second nature to me. I could tell this wasn't going well. Everything they were doing was making him more and more angry. A little more than an hour before lunchtime, I finally intervened.

I went over to Richard and lifted him up. He bristled in anger. His whole body was wound tight. His face was red, his arms and legs were spring loaded and ready to fight. I rested him on my hip and we walked over to a rocking chair where I sat and held him tight against me. He fought it and tried to get up, but I held him firmly. Slowly and gently, I rocked him. I started humming to him the tune from *Jesus loves Me*.

After a few minutes his little body went limp and he started to relax with his head on my chest.

After a while, I asked him, "Why are you so mad today?"

He said, "Mimi, I miss Dad." (All the kids at the daycare called me "Mimi").

I whispered, "I know buddy. You'll see him again."

He said, "I never know when I'm going to see my Dad."

Wow! That was quite a tug on the heartstrings.

Déjà vu. I know exactly how this boy feels.

I composed myself then told him, "I'm sorry you are so sad today. It's even okay to be mad but hitting the other kids is wrong."

His face relaxed and he nodded.

I continued, "The other kids here are your friends."

I continued to sit and rock and hum for a long time. The other kids continued to play all around us. The staff brought the kids to the lunchroom and served lunch while the two of us simply rocked back and forth. After a couple of hours, his little head popped up. He decided he was okay and asked, "Can I get lunch?"

I said, "Richard, we love you and we are your friends. You can talk to us any time."

He asked, "Mimi, will you rock me and hum to me even if I'm not sad?"

I said, "Any time for as long as you need me to."

He smiled and we hugged, then he climbed down and ran off to eat his lunch. He was fine the rest of the day.

The daycare was the most rewarding six years of my life. I felt like it was my way of giving back for what people like Margaret the piano lady, my teacher Mrs. Freitag, and so many more had done for me when I was a kid.

However, not everything was perfect. While I was working at the daycare, I reached down to pick up a child and my head started pounding. I was familiar with headaches, they were unwelcome visitors my whole life, but this one was worse than before. A pulsating drum throbbed in the back of my head all day long. When I went home, I took a couple of aspirin but nothing changed. When I awoke the next day the pounding continued. It was more than just a headache, everything hurt. The overhead lights seemed to be too bright, I was nauseous and wanted to vomit. I couldn't handle sunshine at all. Every loud noise, dropped toy, or scream brought another wave of pain to my head. It was all I could do to just get through the day. It continued until the following day when I finally had relief. Then, a few days later, it started all over again.

After having this sequence of events transpire over and over again, I discovered the true definition of a migraine headache. Like an unwelcome guest, they came back whenever they wanted and lasted anywhere from a day to half a week. They would start as a headache and if I didn't get on top of it in time it went into a full-blown migraine. My head would pound. I often had slurred speech. A number of times, the staff working at the daycare thought I was having a stroke. On really bad days even I passed out from the pain. On a couple of occasions, I passed out in the daycare bathroom. My staff wanted to help, and one of them always sat with me, knowing that I'd come around. I instructed them, "If this happens again, leave me alone. If you call 911, I'll fire you." They joked about it, but they knew I was serious.

I went to doctors and chiropractors. I had MRIs but it always came back to one thing – the trauma from my past. They explained to me that migraine headaches are vascular in nature. They told me that my brain was changing with age and it was pushing down on my cerebellum. When my blood vessels expanded with a headache, it increased pressure and this lead to a migraine. They also said my brain was no longer producing an adequate amount of the chemical called serotonin. They prescribed medications including a serotonin booster. I learned over time to manage them and their frequency decreased. I cherished the headache free days.

When I had a bad headache, I wanted someone to be with me at home. Chris was always caring and gentle. I loved having him home, but if he couldn't be there, he called Jan. She knew the migraines scared me so she dropped everything she was doing and came over to stay with me. In her loving gentleness, she sat with me and rocked back and forth with me and prayed.

The headaches were so vivid, the pounding in my head was so audible and overwhelming, I imagined that certainly Jan must be able hear it too. I asked Jan, "Can you could hear the drums playing inside my head?"

"No, I can't," she said.

After this went on for a few weeks, she realized that I would be comforted if she agreed. When I asked, "Can you hear the drums?"

She said, "Yes, I can hear them." For some reason that made me feel better.

One beautiful sunny morning, I awoke without a headache. I sat up in bed and smiled. I went to the kitchen sink and looked out the window, thrilled to see the sun. Then I sat down on the kitchen table and wrote out my thoughts for the day:

A View of the Sun

My head does not hurt today. I was standing at the kitchen sink this morning doing dishes from last night. Normally I stand at that same sink in front of that same window and shut the sun out. Most days the sun seems to be my enemy. Its piercing rays force their way through the shiny clear glass and the sharp rays of brightness make me cringe in pain as they invade the innermost depths of my head. The pain forces its way quickly to the back of my head and the drums start to play an awful tune, a victory over its captor. I quickly seal my eyes shut in surrender. I can hear the drums pounding in my head, I can see a kaleidoscope of colored flashing behind my thin eyelids and for a brief moment stand in a paralyzed state. The ensemble continues to play its chant of torture for hours on end and some days never giving a hint of reprieve.

Today was different. I stood at that same window of doom and welcomed the rays of sunshine. I stood with my face to the sun and felt the warmth of its rays on my pale face. The heat encompassed every aura of my body like a giant hug you never want to let go of. Today, it was comforting and relaxing as if the rays were apologizing for the pain of the past mornings. They are kind today, only stopping at the edge of my glossy blue eyes. I could have stood there for hours forgiving and forgetting what they have done to me in the past and welcoming with open arms the hope they bring me today.

A few days later, Jan and I met for coffee. It had been a couple of days since a headache and I was feeling fine, but I was living in fear of another headache returning at any time. In my frustration, I told Jan, "My health issues never seem to end. I feel like God is punishing me."

She asked, "Why do you say that?"

I said, "I just feel like I am still suffering the repercussions of what my dad had done to me."

She asked about my dad and I gave her a short summary of my story, including some of the things I suffered at my father's hand. She wasn't scared off by my story, rather she cried with me.

I asked her, "I know God says to consider it pure joy when we go through trials of many kinds."

She smiled, "You're quoting the first chapter of James."

I shrugged, "I haven't seen that happen. When is God going to start turning my trials into joy?"

She gracefully smiled back, "When you start believing!"

I shook my head, "Start believing what?"

She explained, "Anyone can call themselves a Christian but it means nothing until you make him the Lord of your life and follow Jesus in obedience."

She paused for a moment to let that sink in. I said, "I've been in church all my life. Of course I'm a Christian."

She asked, "Why do you say that?"

I said, "I prayed a prayer when I was a little girl in Sunday School."

150

She said, "In the New Testament, there are lots of times when the Gospel is explained. A number of episodes when people turn to Jesus and receive salvation, but we never see in the Bible anyone saying, 'Repeat these words after me.' Nowhere in the Bible does it say, 'Pray this prayer with me.' Or even the most common phrase, 'Ask Jesus into your heart.' Those aren't in the Bible."

I was shocked.

She continued, "Jesus' ministry was teaching people to repent and believe. Salvation certainly involves crying out for God to save you, but also believing in Jesus as your savior."

I nodded in agreement.

Jan said, "In the Bible, the book of Romans does say that everyone who calls out to the Lord will be saved. So at some level, salvation definitely involves prayer and calling out to God for redemption. But that doesn't mean a simple, 'Repeat these words after me' type of prayer turns you into a follower of Christ. It would be wise to be as Biblical as possible in the way we call people to follow Christ. To be a follower of Jesus is to repent from a sinful life, to turn from sin, to have brokenness over sin. It's to trust and believe in Jesus as Savior and Lord. And trust in Jesus as King over our lives. He is the King over the nations and the universe."

I was frustrated, "I'm definitely broken. I've turned from sin. But I'm still hurting from everything my dad did to me."

Her eyes showed her love and she was gentle with her words. "You need to forgive your Dad, but first you need to believe that you are forgiven."

I was dumbfounded.

Forgive my Dad?

Did she really just say that?

Did she hear my story? Does she understand what my dad did?

Jan said, "I know it might not make sense right now, but when you are able to forgive him for what he did, that will change everything."

I had no words.

She can't be serious.

Jan prayed with me that day, "Jesus, please help Ramie. Let her know that she is loved and that she is forgiven."

I bristled knowing that she was about to talk about Dad.

She continued, "Also, help Ramie to start the process of forgiving her Dad."

Start the process? What does that mean?

I said, "I thought forgiving someone was something you just did."

She gave me a hug and we talked a bit more. For the next several days I thought about what she had said. I believed I was forgiven. Jesus was real to me. But I was also confused.

How do you forgive someone who hurt you so deeply?

How do you forgive someone who never said that they were sorry?

Chapter 19

I struggled with the concept of forgiving Dad for a couple of months. It was eating me up inside. Every memory was torture. Every thought of him brought back pain.

One time when we visited, I said, "I just don't see how I can forgive my Dad."

Jan said, "Forgiveness is a big topic. A lot of people think that if they forgive someone that means things will be peachy afterwards, all consequences of their actions are gone."

I said, "Right."

She said, "Some say that you only need to forgive someone if they ask for your forgiveness.

I shrugged, "I guess so."

She continued, "Some think that if you forgive another person, suddenly you love and trust them completely."

I didn't know what to say.

She continued, "None of this is true."

I asked, "What do you mean?"

Jan said, "Forgiving someone is not a magical way to re-establish a relationship. It doesn't mean that you have to trust them again."

I said, "That's a relief."

She said, "It's a change in your heart, but doesn't alter their side of the equation. They don't have to ask for forgiveness for you to forgive them."

I blurted out, "My dad doesn't deserve to be forgiven!"

Jan opened her Bible and read, "I'm gonna read something to you." She flipped open the oversized book with a fancy leather cover. "It doesn't matter if he deserves to be forgiven." She found the spot she was looking for and read, "In Colossians chapter three and verse thirteen, Paul tells the church in Colossae, 'Bear with each other and forgive one another if any of you has a grievance against someone. Forgive as the Lord forgave you'. Those are powerful words."

I was silent. I didn't know how to do that.

Jan said, "Just think about what it means to forgive as the Lord forgave you. What does that mean?"

I didn't like what she was saying. I didn't deserve to be forgiven either. I just wouldn't say it.

Every night I prayed. I prayed over my boys, I asked God to help Chris at his job, and I slipped in something about trying to forgive Dad.

A couple of weeks later, we met again. I let her know that I had thought about it a lot but wasn't ready to do what she said I needed to. Jan never seemed to go anywhere without her Bible, it was in her lap while we talked. She started flipping the onionskin pages as she spoke and said, "We don't deserve Jesus to forgive us."

I said, "I know."

She gently landed on her page and read, "Do not judge, and you will not be judged. Do not condemn, and you will not be condemned. Forgive and you will be forgiven."

I was surprised, "I've heard the do not judge part plenty over the years, but I didn't realize that it was right alongside the instruction to forgive."

Jan said, "That's Luke chapter six, verse thirty seven."

I said, "Thanks." I wrote down the reference. I tried to keep track of everything she told me.

She continued, "So it's not just a suggestion. Jesus is giving this as a command."

She flipped a few more pages and read again, "In Mark chapter eleven, verse twenty five we hear Jesus say, 'And when you stand praying, if you hold anything against anyone, forgive them, so that your Father in heaven may forgive you your sins.'" She paused to make sure I was taking in the full dose of what she was dealing out. She continued, "Then there is the instruction in the book of Matthew, my favorite."

I made notes while she flipped her pages.

She read, "For if you forgive other people when they sin against you, your heavenly Father will also forgive you. That's Matthew six, fourteen."

I closed my eyes and shook my head. Jan meant well, but I just didn't get it. I countered, "But he's dead!"

She put a hand on my shoulder, "Ramie, look at me."

I opened my eyes and a tear fell to the floor.

She said, "He doesn't seem dead, to me. Based on what you are going through, he's alive and well." She laid her hand gently on my face then pointed at my temple. "In here."

I agreed, "Very much."

She said, "If he lived far away and you weren't able to communicate with him, you could still forgive him. Forgiveness is something you do in your heart. It doesn't matter if he is alive or dead. It's your heart changing in relation to him."

She continued, "When you ask Jesus to forgive you, He does. If you sin again, and once again repent and ask for forgiveness, what does he do?"

I said, "He forgives."

She said, "What does Jesus say about forgiving people over and over again?"

I said, "Are you talking about the time when Jesus says something about seventy times seven?"

She flipped her pages again and landed on Matthew eighteen, twenty-two. "Peter came up and said to him, "Lord how often will my brother sin against me, and I forgive him? As many as seven times?' Jesus said to him, "I do not say to you seven times, but seventy times seven times."

I said, "I've heard that plenty of times. I know it's not a math problem."

She nodded, "It's not a number. We don't need to pull out a calculator. It just means lots and lots."

I finally acquiesced and was determined to start the process of forgiving my Dad. Forgiving my dad was the right thing to do. Not because he deserved it, but because it was right. Even if we don't feel like it, we need to take the step in obedience and forgive.

I asked Jan, "But where do I start?

Jan said, "You're a visual person, right?"

I said, "Absolutely, I do best with things I can see, touch and feel."

She said, "Then it needs to be visual. Out in front of you so you can see it. Take some time and write a letter to your Dad."

I asked, "A letter? Like an old fashioned one you put in the mail with a stamp?"

She said, "Yes, write out 'Dear Dad' and make it a letter like people get in the mail. Be specific, tell him as much as you can."

So the next day I took some time by myself when I was alone at home and sat down at the kitchen table and took a pen to paper. At the top of the page I wrote, "Dear Dad," just like Jan told me to. Then I hesitated. I had revealed some of the things that happened to Dr. Reichman when he asked me if I had been in a terrible accident. There were other things that I had told Chris. But there was so much to tell, so much that I had never told anybody.

I put down my pen and cried.

The next day I struggled to pick up the pen once again and managed to get out a couple of sentences. Every stroke of the pen brought with it a flood of emotions. This process was even more involved than the days in the hospital after I heard that he had passed away.

I wrote the letter over the course of several days. Every moment of the process was a struggle. Sometimes I couldn't write anything at all. It was all I could do to get out of bed and cry. Then, the next day, I began writing again. I wrote down on paper everything I could possibly think of. All the times he hurt me physically emotionally, and mentally. It was a heart wrenching experience.

When I was finished, I called Jan. "I've written the letter. What do we do next?"

She said, "I'll be right over."

Together we sat on the couch and I held the letter in my hands. "Go ahead," she said. "Read it."

I read it out loud, every word from beginning to end. Each incident that I read about was awful and painful: tying me to the bed, Pandy, eating disorders, drain cleaner, killing Grandma, and on and on. Many of these experiences I had never before shared with anybody before. Sharing the stories was painful but freeing for me. After reading those terrible words that recounted the horrific experiences I actually felt better. Speaking it out loud with my trusted friend and mentor somehow helped it lose the power that it held over me. I had spoken the truth and the truth was setting me free. No longer did I have to bear that burden alone. That was comforting.

I set the papers down on the table and closed my eyes. I knew what was coming next, but I didn't know if I had the strength to do it.

I said, "Lord Jesus, I ask for your forgiveness and for the ability to help me forgive Dad."

Jan said, "Go back through the letter and read it once again. This time, take a few minutes after each line and forgive him."

I did as she instructed. I read a line and stopped. I remembered the offense, as clearly as I was able and pondered what it did to me. Then I read a little more, and stopped. Eventually, I was able to speak the words out loud.

I said, "I forgive you for not being there for me."

Jan held my hand.

I said, "I forgive you for not protecting me."

Jan whispered quietly, "Keep going."

As I went down the letter, I progressed to the more painful memories. I said, "I forgive you for hurting me."

Jan rocked back and forth with me. We waited a few minutes. There was no rush. Jan was patient with me.

We continued in this manner one line at a time. It was not quick or easy. Every line was full of turmoil. But once we got the ball rolling, it seemed to get easier. We persisted until we reached the end of the letter.

I said, "I forgive you for killing my grandma."

Jan said, "You're doing great."

I sat in a puddle of tears.

Jan and I talked and cried. Then we talked some more and cried some more. Finally, we prayed.

She gently took the stack of papers and folded them. She gave me a manila envelope and said, "Let's mail it."

I wrote out the address of the house I grew up in and provided no return address. We took it to the post office. They weighed the package and I paid the postage and sent it off. I felt like I was walking on air. That was one of the most liberating things I had ever done. I felt a freedom that I had never felt before.

I have no idea what happened to the letter. I don't know if it reached it's destination or if it was lost in the mail. I don't know if anyone got it and read it or if they sent it back to the post office.

For years I had asked God, "Why do I suffer?" I didn't realize it, but I was playing the victim. I was saying "Poor me. I was abused."

Now, after having gone through the process of forgiveness, I claimed victory in Jesus Christ. He has set me free to forgive and move on.

Yes, I still have pain.

Back pain, pain in my wrists, and the occasional migraine headache. They are constant reminders of Dad. With every reminder that I encounter, I have to forgive him again. For me, forgiving Dad is almost a daily task.

Looking down at my wrists, I had a vivid reminder of my past. Scars from my suicide attempts were slightly visible to my friends, but to me, they screamed about my late teenage years. The crooked bones that my dad broke had never been set. The constant reminder that I saw every moment when I looked at my hands was something that I could change. I imagined a way to see something positive when I looked at my own skin. I wanted the old memories covered with something beautiful and positive.

I had always been fascinated with sunflowers. They are tolerant of heat and droughts – a strong, feminine flower. The center is full of seeds, which have tremendous potential. The sunflower is rich in symbolism.

I took my ideas to a tattoo shop and communicated to them what I wanted. I had my forearms emblazoned with images of sunflowers with golden petals. The first flower represents God's hands holding my life. The subsequent flowers are His blessings raining down on me from heaven.

My physical scars are covered. No longer do I see the pain of the past, but rather the beauty of the future.

When we forgive, we don't change the past but we certainly can change our future.

Chapter 20

While my boys were playing outside, I watched them through the kitchen window as I fixed dinner when suddenly my world changed with a simple phone call. I answered and the voice on the other end said, "Is the Sara Smith?"

I paused and replied, "Who is this?"

A female voice on the other end of the line said, "This is the adult social service department in Omaha, Nebraska."

I said, "That used to be my name but I go by Ramie now, and I'm married so my last name is now Stenzel. How did you get my number?"

She said, "I'm working with your mother. She told me your name had been changed so we looked you up."

I grimaced at the thoughts of my mother. Painful memories poured into my mind. I tried to be polite, "Okay. How can I help you?"

The voice said, "You mother is no longer mentally capable of making decisions for herself. We need to know if you would agree to sign on as her guardian."

I was shocked, "You're kidding, right?"

She said, "Not at all, ma'am. If you agree to sign on as guardian, you would be the one to make decisions on her well-being instead of the State of Nebraska. At the social services office, we try to keep these decisions in the hands of family. Mrs. Stenzel, are you willing to sign on guardianship of your mother?"

I replied, "I don't even know my mother."

I sat in a silent shock. My mind drifted back to the courtroom all those years ago. I remembered watching my mom cry from the witness stand as she showed no sign of wanting to fight for her children. Then I remembered trying to hug her, and my arms slipping out from around her neck...

The voice came again, "Mrs. Stenzel, are you willing to sign on guardianship of your mother?"

My mind came back to the present. I replied in a somber voice, "Listen, if you're calling in regards to my mother, then you have access to my file as well. If you read that, you'll find that I don't know my mother."

The lady urged, "But she is your mother."

I shook my head. My mother didn't fight for me and made all the wrong decisions for me as a child. Now I was being asked to be an advocate for her and make decisions for her well being. I knew she couldn't see my gestures over the phone, but my hands were up in the air with palms up saying, "It's not my problem!" I heard my voice say, "I can't. I'm sorry, but I can't."

The lady was confused by my response and she said she could call me back in a week and give me some time to think about it.

I made a journal entry that day and processed the phone call. After thinking about it for a while, the words spilled on the page:

Stranger's Voice

There is a strangely familiar voice
That races through my head
One so recently found
And not quite sure if I dread
Her voice is a curious danger
That disturbs my eager heart
She is a troubled distant stranger
Only wanting a brand-new start
My heart is drawn to
Her mesmerizing tune
My mind says to back off
And leave her well alone
She echoes a comforting sound
That is heard from a mother's womb

A voice unlike all others
Engraved in my memory
Taken to my eternal tomb
It's a bond between mother and child
One that can never be broken
Even through the years of lives unreconciled
I still know her voice
With only one spoken word

The call came the following week once again. In a very short conversation, she asked again. I didn't have to think about it this time, I simply said no. A week later, I declined again. After a few weeks, the calls stopped coming.

Thoughts of my mother consumed me. Mom promised Dad that a baby would make her better. I was planned. I was wanted. I was conceived on Valentines Day 1969. But that promise wasn't kept. The presence of another baby didn't make my mom better; instead I made her worse. That was my personal back-story that I heard growing up. Both of my parents made sure I knew that. I failed my mom as much as she had failed me.

The social worker called again about four months later. I recognized her right away, but this time her demeanor was different. "Ramie, I need to talk to you."

I launched into my defense stance, "I already told you I'm not signing the papers."

She replied, "You don't have to. Your mom found out you denied the papers. She went into a deep depression. I don't know how to tell you this."

I asked, "Tell me what?"

She said, "I'm sorry, but she took her own life."

I had no response.

After all the years of trying, my mother was finally successful in a suicide attempt.

She said, "I'm sorry to have to be the one to bring you this news."

I closed my eyes and shook my head.

She asked, "Do you want a copy of the death certificate?"

I said, "No."

She said, "She has a limited number of belongings ..."

I said, "No, I didn't want anything."

I had resigned myself to that fact a long time before. I had concluded that I wasn't supposed to have a mom. I never went to mother/daughter functions. I figured if God wanted me to have a mom, He would have given me one – a real one!

She was gone. There was no more wondering if she would show up on my doorstep being normal. There was no more wondering if she thought of me on my birthday, or if she even remembered it.

I retreated to my journal and once again the words flowed:

Memories of a Song

I try so hard to escape the memories
Running rampant through my mind
So many thoughts and feelings
Also awkwardly intertwined
My mind is a place I cannot escape
No matter how hard I try
It unforgivingly plays tape after tape
And all I can do is cry
I close my eyes and see her face
I lay my head upon her chest
And then my heart begins to race
She hums the notes to a classical tune
While her heart echoes a different beat
I know the song will be ending soon
And this chapter of my life complete
I pray the lord will be gentle and kind
As his love starts renewing my mind
I lay my head upon His chest
As He sings a new song to me
I will put my memories of her to rest
And allow the Lord to set me free

I grieved and grieved hard. Not the typical type of grieving that most people do. I grieved for what I never had and always had wanted and needed. I was angry at my mom for not being the mother I needed her to be. I was angry at God for not giving me someone to share my hopes and dreams with, to go shopping with, to have lunch dates with. I had nobody to snuggle up with and watch movies and eat junk food. I had nobody to pray with me, encourage me, and speak God's word over my life.

Why didn't God think I deserved that?

I took my Mom's death hard. I waivered in my faith. It didn't take long to fall back into my old ways of numbing the pain that I felt. I felt rejected and robbed of the mom I so desperately needed.

That night after the kids went to bed I mixed a strong drink and sat on the couch. It had been years since I had imbibed, so it didn't take much to take my mind off my mother. I didn't get drunk, but in my swirling emotions I retreated to my old standby. The following night, I revisited alcohol for an escape. Day by day, I began slipping into an unhealthy manner of dealing with problems.

A few months passed and as I sat in church I heard the announcement for our annual Ladies' Retreat. Every year, 40-45 ladies from the church made our way to a retreat center about two hours from home. We had a handful of little traditions: we stopped at the same place for lunch and shopped at a few thrift stores along the way. It was generally a fun time together. Usually, the church brought in a speaker who promised to teach and inspire us. I had no desire to get closer to God. I signed up as an excuse to get away from life for a couple of days. We traveled to the retreat center and I settled into my cabin with the other ladies.

That night, our speaker was introduced. Her name was Kelly Randles, the wife of evangelist Jon Randles, from just outside Dallas Texas. Kelly was a petite lady with fiery red hair and energy to match. Kelly was a Texas tornado. She was on fire for the Lord and as she took the stage, I couldn't help but be drawn to her. She was so full of joy! She taught from the Bible and though I wasn't expecting to be drawn in, I hung on every word of her Texas drawl.

I sat in the back during the first session wearing my favorite hoodie and baseball cap. Kelly was funny. She said a couple of statements that piqued my interest. As I went back to my room that night, my heart was aching and the things Kelly said were knocking on my heart.

Kelly's version of the story:

The first time I saw Ramie, she was holding up a wall of windows, leaning back in a chair. She was wearing an oversized pink hooded sweatshirt, with the hood pulled up over her to keep intruders from entering her "space." Upon closer inspection, she was also wearing a pink baseball cap under the pink hoodie, as if the cap's bill created an extra line of defense against would-be friends. Her arms were crossed to protect her heart. I was taken aback somewhat by her demeanor; it didn't seem like she wanted to be at the Women's Retreat nor like she wanted any vulnerability with God or with people.

As I taught that night, I noticed her sitting up in her chair on occasion. She seemed surprised that I would say that each of us shows the character of God imprinted in our temperament.

For the second session, she sat in the middle section at the back, no longer hugging the wall but still out of arm's length. Her pink hoodie was down, revealing long blonde braids coming out of the pink ball cap. She was beautiful, radiant … to me.

Back to my room that night, Kelly's words reverberated in my mind. I knew God was doing something. But I wasn't going to let that happen. I brought along some alcohol shooters with me just for this reason and made use of them in my room that night. The following morning, I woke up feeling rested and calm. No hangover, just relaxed and ready to face the day.

I waited for the morning session to begin and sat out in the common area in a rocking chair crocheting an afghan. Kelly had been staying in a separate building. I was surprised to see her walk in. She approached and pulled up a chair right in front of me and watched me crochet. My hands kept moving in rhythmic motions maneuvering the yarn into delicate knots to make the blanket. She watched me create my masterpiece.

She said, "That looks beautiful."

I smiled.

She asked, "Who are you making it for?"

She was sincere in her questions. I answered, "I don't know yet. I'm always working on one of these."

She really cares about me.

Why is this lady that I don't even know taking such interest in me and what I was doing?

I found it odd yet intriguing. We talked for a while and I enjoyed our conversation. Though it had nothing to do with her presentation or the gospel message that she normally shares, I felt like we connected. She excused herself and went to do her microphone check before the morning session. I gathered my things and got there early to get my seat in the back.

Her second talk was just as interesting as the first. We broke for lunch and had some free time in the afternoon.

Kelly came over once again and asked another series of questions about my afghans.

"I've got a finished one in my room."

She said, "I'd love to see it."

She followed me to my room. I sat on the edge of my bed as I rummaged through my bag and found the afghan I was looking for. I pulled it out and draped it across the corner of the bed. She stood in front of me. I thought she was going to ask me more questions, about the afghan, about what I thought about her message, about the retreat center. Anything. Instead, she stepped close to me and reached her arms around me and gently embraced me. I laid my head against her chest. I could hear her heartbeat. Part of me wanted to pull away and part of me was actually enjoying being held and I felt a sense of comfort.

She whispered, "You are beautiful."

That's not what I expected you to say.

She said softly, "You are loved."

I sobbed.

She quietly declared, "You are worthy."

I melted into her arms as she gently rocked back and forth.

She pronounced, "You are wanted."

As these words of affirmation were spoken to me, my walls of separation started crumbling around me. I started to cry uncontrollably. Kelly took my ball cap off and kissed me on the top of my head.

Love was a difficult word for me. I knew how to love my husband, the relationship between Chris and I was one of mutual love and respect. I knew how to love my boys in the way that I always wanted to be loved. But I had never felt love like I should have felt from my parents. Neither my mother nor my father ever told me they loved me, or showed it.

I could never let God love me. I didn't feel worthy. I didn't think God loved me.

We sat in my room for about an hour. Kelly hugged me and told me she loved me. She let me cry.

Thoughts from Kelly:

The next day, I had a chance to actually interact with Ramie in the afternoon. The lodge was a long rectangle with a kitchen on one end and rooms on both sides. Each room had two twin beds with a little table in between, so cozy with quilts and blankets at the ready. The central meeting area had lots of tables and chairs that mixed and matched, with comfort as the goal. There were several rocking chairs lining the walls, which is where I found my little sweetheart.

She was hiding under the most beautiful afghan that she was crocheting at the time. I almost didn't see her. She was fast and good! She was quite far along on this gigantic, multicolored afghan, so it draped her as it grew from her fingers. I came over to her to see her, to meet her, because I was drawn to her. I had never had an experience quite like this before. God was choosing me for her, and her for me.

As I approached, she was so timid that I wasn't sure she even wanted the interruption. But as we talked, I discovered that she was a butterfly still in her cocoon ... a little yarn-made cocoon to protect herself.

The more we talked, the more enthralled with her I was. Even though I had three teenagers at home myself, I could see that this woman of thirty-six needed a spiritual momma! My heart was drawn like a magnet to hers but not by my doing; it was the Holy

Spirit putting us together to create a new thing: a spiritual momma showing the love that a real momma should have, in order to allow God to reaffirm to Ramie that, even though He had always been there for her, He would give her the desire of her heart...the flesh and blood arms and heart of someone who loved her unconditionally!

I remember the first time that I just wrapped my arms around her in a big bear hug! We are two completely different sizes: I am short, only five feet tall if I stand up really straight, while she is very tall and looks even taller next to me! So she sat while I tried to give her my best "motherly" hug. She held on to me for dear life! And my heart broke for her. There was no pity in me for her situation, only compassion for this talented, smart, lovely woman who was also an orphan in need of a mother.

By the end of the retreat, it was decided I would adopt her as my spiritual daughter. She has a huge gift for creativity with a heart to give! At that time, long distance calling was quite expensive, in fact, by the minute. Quite quickly we realized that talking on the phone was going to be a difficult and hard-to-schedule luxury. Writing was our best choice for exchanging stories and for Ramie to bare her heart. Sometimes she wrote pages and pages...her gift for writing was evident even then. But like a child, she also wanted to send me things she had made herself.

She began to make the most beautiful and elaborate cards, with the inside sentiment addressed to Momma Kel. Most of the time, her heart needed to share more than the space inside allowed for, so she would include notebook pages full of what she was desperate to share with her "spiritual Momma."

I have kept every single one to this day.

The rest of the weekend retreat was a blur. The remaining sessions came and went and everyone was packing up to head back to the reality of our normal lives and problems. Kelly and I exchanged addresses and phone numbers. She promised we would keep in contact but I had my doubts. She was an evangelist's wife. She speaks to hundreds of ladies a year. I'm sure she meets with troubled ladies all the time.

Why would she keep in contact with me? Besides she was in Texas and I was in Idaho.

A few days later the phone rang, I answered, "Hello?"

"Ramie!"

I instantly recognized her Texas drawl. "Kelly! It's so good to hear from you!"

"How's the afghan coming along?"

I laughed at her basic good-natured southern charm. We talked on the phone for a few minutes and I was refreshed.

I sent her the afghan that I had been working on at the retreat. We talked and then emailed back and forth for several weeks. Kelly spoke Jesus to me and I started to grow in my relationship with the Lord once again. I was intrigued by her wisdom and her joy. She understood me. She really wanted to be a part of my life. She brought a positive and productive twist that I rarely saw in people. After we hung up, I looked forward to speaking with her again.

I could tell from our time together that she didn't pay attention to every conference attendee like she did to me. I still couldn't wrap my head around the fact that I was the one she picked. I was still holding back and kept some distance in my heart. My mom had committed suicide. It seemed that Kelly was too good to be true and I feared she would stop being my friend if she found out how wounded I really was. Of course, Mrs. Kelly wasn't born yesterday. She somehow knew that there was much more going on in my life than I allowed people to see. She patiently kept talking with me until I felt comfortable enough to tell her. Or scare her away.

I asked, "Why are you spending so much time with me?"

She said, "I didn't pick you, God did!"

It was clear that the Lord had instructed Kelly to talk with me. I needed her. She listened with the patience of Job. She was to be my spiritual momma. At that point, when we spoke, I started calling her Momma Kel. Then, I opened up to Kelly and told her about my Mom's suicide. We talked for hours and I told her everything! I hated my mom and everything that she wasn't. I still grieved for what I never had had always wanted. As I spoke, I realized that even though I didn't intend to do so, I was once again playing the victim.

168

Every negative thing I ever said about myself to her was immediately thrown into the pit of hell and replaced with the word of God and how He sees me as His child. She said, "I am fearfully and wonderfully made. Thank you for making me so wonderfully complex! Your workmanship is marvelous – how well I know it."

I knew she was quoting the Bible. I asked, "Where is that from?

She said, "Honey, it's Psalm 139 verse 14."

I said, "It's beautiful."

Kelly said, "You will never be able to move forward until you forgive your Mom."

The words hit me like a bomb. I knew what this meant. I had been through the process with my Dad, and now with my Mom, it would be just as tough. But I knew she was right.

Kelly continued, "But first you have to let go of the hurt and the broken little girl inside you."

How did she know that I had left that broken little girl in my rear-view mirror so many years ago?

She said, "All that hurt you have stuffed deep down and ignored for so many years. You need to bring that little girl out."

I cried as she spoke.

This would be quite different than the process of dealing with my Dad.

She continued, "Let's find that little girl. You needed to let her pain come out. You need to cry with her, calm her fears, heal her hurts. Forgive her and set her free. You need to forgive yourself and let the inner child go."

It took a few long talks, a lot of writing, and Kelly praying with me to do all of that. I filled a spiral bound notebook with thoughts. At first they were random, then they became organized, eventually they morphed into poetic dances on the page.

Sunflower Fields

I run as a child through sunflower fields
I am free and wild I feel the warmth of His hand
I smell the fragrance of him

Yet I am hurt and torn
Some days wonder why I was born
He says He chose me before I came to be
His plan was for me to be free

Free to love and to be loved
To always look to Him above
He looks down on me from Heaven
He sees me dance as if I were still seven

He extends His arms down to pick me up
I raise my hands to surrender
My pain I will no longer remember
He holds me tight
I melt into His loving arms
Never to put up a fight

I am comforted
I am safe
And I will always yield to Him
For He will always be
At the end of my sunflower field

When it was all down on paper, I had the freedom to move on.
Over the phone, Kelly explained to me that Mom didn't have some
mental capacity to be what I needed her to be. She made me see Mom
for who she was and what she had been through. Mom was abused as
a child herself. She didn't ask for that either. She had things happen to
her that were out of her control. She didn't have anyone to ask for
help except for doctors so she dealt with her past the only way she
knew how, drugs. She didn't have a church family, a relationship with
God, or any type of mentor.

I felt myself grieving at a deeper level. I never had to put
words to the last time I saw her. I was upset that Mom didn't fight for
me, but as Kelly showed me more and more about her, my focus
shifted. I began to be upset that she couldn't fight! She didn't have the
skill set to launch a social justice fight for her children. I felt the pain

that she must have felt in losing me and knowing that she may never hug me again, hum to me, or let me sit on her lap.

Mom didn't ask for the life that she was handed. She didn't want to lose her kids. She had no choice. When I put myself in her shoes for a while, I knew that if I had been in her situation with all her upbringing and teaching, I would have done the same things she did. Many of us would have.

I cried for hours. Kelly listened and prayed with me.

I knew Mom's pain. I knew the pain of separation and abuse. We shared the same pain yet we both chose to deal with it differently. Mom chose drugs and prostitution. By this point in my life, I could stand firmly and declare that I chose the Lord to break the generational chains of the past and to be different. Kelly loved and accepted me for who I was and where I was. In our time together, she had shown me a tremendous amount of empathy. My hatred for my mom had transformed into a deep compassion for her. With Kelly's coaching, I grew in my perception of my mom. I began to have tenderness towards her and was building an understanding of who she was and what she had been through.

I loved my mom.

In time I was able to forgive her. In doing so, I set the little girl inside me free. It wasn't a process of writing it all out and listing the offenses and forgiving them one by one. This was different from my Dad. It was simply a matter of knowing her as a person and loving her. Once that happened, forgiving her was the most natural thing in the world. With Kelly on the phone, I forgave Mom easily and calmly.

I had harbored bitterness against her for so long, a wall had separated us. I thought back on my refusal to be her legal guardian and her resulting suicide. I felt terrible for my own actions.

Then an amazing thing happened. Once I had forgiven Mom, my heart softened. I was able to take a step back and see it all through God's perspective. Our Father in heaven is incredible. He fills the voids with His love. He holds us in His lap. He hugs us and sings over us with joy! I'm a full-grown lady now, and still fit in His lap! Somehow, through the process of forgiveness, God opened up a deeper level of worship that I had never experienced before.

I had been wrong in my decisions, but I looked at her totally differently now. God's grace allowed me to see her differently and, subsequently, I was then able to move past my own sin and forgive myself. Under Kelly's guidance I was able to think through my own actions in a new way. Yes, I was wrong. And yes, Jesus forgives. Yes, so do I.

I imagined all the best of my mother. She was a hummer. Her humming comforted me when I was little. I pictured a hummingbird surrounded by musical notes. A tattoo artist brought the image to life with a hummingbird approaching the sunflower on my right forearm.

On my left forearm, just above a sunflower is a permanent sketch of a little girl in a sundress releasing a handful of balloons. The words, "Letting go" float under the rising balloons as a constant reminder to me to let go of my past.

Forgiveness isn't easy. Sometimes the process of forgiving can be even more painful than the initial offense we suffered. Yet there is no peace without forgiveness.

Chapter 21

Kelly and I continued have a sweet friendship over the next few months. It was clear to me by now she really wasn't going anywhere. She continued to show me the unconditional love of a spiritual momma. She spoke words of affirmation to me. She knew that I still struggled. Over and over again, she told me that she loved me. She told me that God loved me. I knew this on a surface, educational Sunday-School level. But I struggled to internalize it.

This dovetailed with my myriad of self-esteem issues. I was my own worst enemy and a lot of the time. I talked negatively about myself frequently but Mrs. Kelly wouldn't have it. She shot down every negative thing that I said about myself and replaced it with something positive. She told me I was loved and deserved to live. I was worthy of God's love. I was worthy of my husband's love. And I was worthy of my three rowdy babies. I was able to provide for them a happy healthy life.

God picked Mrs. Kelly because he knew she would have to be stern and honest and show me some tough love. He knew I would receive it from her.

Kelly returned to Idaho to speak at one of the local churches. Of course, I showed up in my hoodie and ball cap. Kelly got to meet Chris and the boys and they got to spend some time together. She loved our dogs as she was an owner of two small dogs herself. Kelly noticed that I had grown a lot. I was no longer wallowing in self-hatred and depression. I had forgiven Mom and was growing in my relationship with Christ, but Kelly saw through me. I was still lacking in the self-esteem areas. After some talking, she asked me if I wanted to come see her in Texas for a few days. I excitedly agreed and we set a date and bought the ticket.

She also told me that she had just put her dog down. At that time, Chris and I were breeding Maltese dogs. We had two females and one stud as family pets. We enjoyed taking care of the litters and regularly sold them. This provided a little supplemental income until the boys were old enough that I could go back to work full time. Kelly was also a dog lover and she always asked lots of questions about our dogs.

I empathized with her and let her know we were about to have another litter. "If you want, I would be happy to give you one of our puppies."

She said, "Oh bless your heart!"

Before I left, Kelly called me on the phone and said, "Pack light."

I said, "I was just going to bring enough for a couple of days."

She said, "Don't bring much clothing. Just come for fun. I want you to come out with no expectations!"

It was an odd request but I agreed. My roller suitcase was mostly empty. I could have brought most of what I had in there in just my purse. I also brought a small pet carrier with a puppy just for Kelly.

I landed in Texas and met Kelly outside the best baggage claim at Dallas Fort Worth International Airport. The hugs were plentiful!!

Kelly's view:

In the Spring of 2008, she came to my house in Texas to give me one of the greatest gifts that I have ever received ... Allegra Sophia Randles, the last of any litter of puppies that Ramie would ever breed. Her mother is full blood Maltese and her father is full blood miniature poodle, so she was so tiny when she arrived, hand delivered by Ramie herself! Chris warned me that they had nicknamed her "The Texas Tornado," and it was the perfect nickname for her! Her markings, as demonstrated in her black and white hair, make her look like she is wearing little white leggings with a black sweater, lined in white! She looks like a darling little aerobics instructor as she plays with her ball all day, doing various exercises to keep herself trim and alert! She watches TV, and barks at every dog that comes on the screen ferociously!!! But, to be fair, I have never been attacked by a dog on TV, so her record is 100%! (Currently, at 11 years old, she is still as trim and spry as the puppy Ramie brought to me all those years ago. We are also inseparable).

Ramie was covered up from head to toe from our first meeting as a sort of visual imperative to stay out of her space! I never felt like that applied to me! She also dressed very boyishly, with oversized shirts or sweatshirts and men's jeans. I could not stay out of her fashion space either, once we met, because I KNEW she was beautiful, not just in some "inner spirit" way, but for real beautiful. Her eyes are a sparkling blue and her blonde hair was long and full when we met. She had a terrible body shaming spirit all around her, and she was so mean to herself! I began to call her on it. Once she started in on herself, I would tell her straight up, "Don't talk about my friend like that! I won't allow that when you're with me!"

She would try to crack jokes about her full figure or call herself fat, and I would not have any of that! She was gorgeous! Her smile lit up the room! She had curves for days and beautiful freckles, but she dressed like Rebecca of Sunnybrook Farm! She always wore her overalls with a long-sleeved shirt and a baggy sweatshirt over it all. She needed to have the woman coaxed out of her, so that she would see that God had made her beautiful, not in some rhetorical way but truly beautiful in a womanly way. She needed to be convinced of that in order for God to truly do a work in her!

The most difficult challenge I had with Ramie was how to introduce true womanhood to her in a way that she would embrace herself as a woman. She treated herself as if she were a 14-year-old tomboy, but was married with three boys and a rowdy husband! Step one was to get the ball cap off. Step two was to get her hair unbraided! Step three was to get her out of her overalls and into something more womanly. That last step proved to be very difficult indeed!

Once her hair was down, it was easy to see that she is gorgeous! When I tried to convince her that being womanly was a good thing, not a bad one, she fought back like a lioness! She honestly didn't want to see herself as beautiful. I am sure that a counselor would see this as a barrier of sorts to all the rejection she had received as a child. Because I was not a psychological expert but instead I was just someone who cared like a good mother should, I just held a strong line of what was truth and what was perception – the truth was that she was and is beautiful. Her perception was that she wasn't a typical beauty so she must not even be pretty.

I was able to get through to her by showing her that her insulting views of herself reflected on Chris. If Chris was a man representing his gender, then he picked a woman he saw as beautiful, and one he continues to desire and have passion for. So by attacking her own view of herself, in essence she was insulting his idea of beauty. She might be mean to herself, but did she really intend to be mean to Chris for finding her attractive?

We spent the next three days eating out, talking, laughing, watching chick flicks in bed, and shopping. I experienced first hand what this proverb meant:

> As iron sharpens iron,
> so one person sharpens another. (Proverbs 27:17)

The shopping was a true experience, like nothing I'd ever been through before. It was a "What Not to Wear Weekend." I wasn't allowed to buy any hoodies. As we shopped, Kelly helped me pick out pretty things. She steered me to clothes that were attractive and some that I never would have picked out for myself.

In the first store at the mall, she handed me a handful of blouses my size and pointed at the changing room. I pulled the first blouse over my head and brushed it smooth, I proudly stepped out of the dressing room and looked in the mirror.

Kelly asked, "Do you feel pretty?"

I looked in the mirror both in front and back and said, "Yes."

Kelly said, "Then we get it."

I went back in and tried on the next one. Again I stepped out and showed off.

Kelly asked, "Do you feel pretty?"

I looked in the mirror and said, "Not this one, no."

Kelly said, "That one goes back on the rack."

We bought everything that made me feel pretty and left the rest. The process continued at the next store. She kept asking me if I felt pretty. By the end of the day, I started to feel pretty and was gaining some confidence in myself. Kelly wasn't trying to change me. She was allowing me to reveal the beauty she saw the inside. The beauty that apparently other people saw ... except me.

More from Momma Kel:

The entire trip was designed to help her make a complete metamorphosis to "womanhood" in a safe environment with me as a Truth Teller. I promised not to placate her as she tried on clothes or put on makeup or picked accessories. I promised instead to tell the Truth in Love. That meant, if it looked ok, I said just that. If it looked terrible, I said just that. But, more often than not, she looked stunning and happy. She shined from the outside in and back out again. It didn't take long until she learned how to pick out what she knew she would like to wear. Her clothes were whites and pastels and flowy and flowery!

I gave her a pearl necklace and I told her, "Every girl gets a pearl necklace from her mother when she is woman enough to wear it." (I am willing to admit that may be something we just do in the South, but it is a tradition nonetheless).

Her creative bent with making cards and afghans and quilts made the mixing and matching of colors and patterns easier for her than for me! Her suitcase was fairly empty when she came, but it was full when she left!

Another thing that I wanted to do as her spiritual Momma Kel was to do for her what I would do for my own kids: every year I gave my kids a Christmas ornament and Christmas pajamas. To be honest, my mother was the one who started the tradition of Christmas pajamas with me as a little girl. For several years after, I would send warm but womanly Christmas pajamas and an ornament for my girl.

She is a gift from God to me, and I am so grateful that she is still in my life!

In time, I started to see my own inner beauty and started to love who I was. I even started to believe that I was worthy to be loved. I started to see myself through God's eyes!

At the end of the weekend, my roller bag was packed full for the ride home. As we headed back to the airport, I had an entirely new outlook on life.

It's been a number of years since I met Kelly. We still talk often and see each other when we can. Chris and I spent our 25th wedding anniversary in Texas. I love Momma Kel and I am thankful for her obedience to the Lord and for the time and wisdom she has invested in me.

I am a life changed.

Chapter 22

Over the years I have dealt with a lot of issues, not the least of which has been food. As a tortured teenager I was a measly 115 pounds. After high school, I gained weight to a healthy 175 pounds. My protruding bones disappeared and I had a comfortable padding over my body. The bones that Dad broke in anger were hidden and protected. My fat was a rebellion of sorts.

They call it an eating disorder. The doctors have lots of fancy names for it: bulimia nervosa, anorexia nervosa, purging disorder, avoidant/restrictive food intake disorder, obsessive-compulsive disorder, food addiction, and my personal favorite eating disorder not otherwise specified. But for me, these were all linked to Dad. He was dead and gone. I had gone through the painful and humbling process of forgiving him. Yet, he was still there. My habits and proclivities had his stamp on me.

Things that I buried for years were creeping up. I didn't have the strength to hold them down any longer. Fear had totally consumed me. I was afraid of failing, afraid of dying, afraid of what else might rear its ugly head. Maybe I wasn't ready to deal with this yet.

I was angry at God. This was the one thing that hit so deep for so many years, I was afraid of reverting back to my old ways. Now that I was working on my diet, I just lost total control over the one thing that I had control over.

As our family grew, I spent plenty of time in the kitchen baking. I kept all types of snacks around: pop, chips, Little Debbie snacks. We were no strangers to fast food. My weight steadily climbed to 240 lbs. Chris struggled as well. The two of us tried dieting in an attempt to get back to a healthy weight. Fad diets were a roller coaster, always ending with giving in and gaining back even more than I had lost.

My self-esteem was low. I was fat and I didn't care. I gave up on myself and quit caring.

Chris and I eventually went to a weight loss doctor together. I lost about 70 pounds and started to see my body take a shape that I had not seen in years. I started to see what had been "broken" and what I had tried to cover up for so long.

I struggled horribly on the inside. When I had a memory from my childhood, I retreated to the comfort of food. With all the internal turmoil, I realized I wasn't ready to let it go. So I gained again.

Although I had come so far, I was still struggling with unresolved issues on the inside. I still continued to stash food, mainly candy. When I was all alone I would pig out. I topped out at an all-time high of 310 pounds.

In January 2018 I began to have some issues with my health. I was tired all the time, lethargic, and just not feeling like myself. This went on for about a week and I felt so ill that I saw a doctor. They did plenty of poking and prodding, hooked me up to an EKG machine, and gave me a stress tests. After the tests were done, he announced, "Ramie, some time in the past week you had a heart attack."

I said, "What?"

He said, "Yours wasn't the type of heart attack that you keel over from right away. We aren't going to do a by-pass or a coronary stent. But we have to recommend some changes in your life."

I was listening.

He continued, "If you don't lose weight and get on a healthier lifestyle, you will have another, more serious heart attack."

His words hit me like a ton of bricks. He laid out a plan for healthy eating and exercise. I was really only given two options: live or die.

I need to address this. Seriously.

Meanwhile Chris was in the process of analyzing his own health. We knew that we had to commit to doing it together. Both of us needed to get healthy. In our household, the word DIET was outlawed

– a four letter word. We had been through various nutrition intake programs and they had failed.

I was struggling on the inside. I had gone up and down in weight many times over the years and had become content and complacent in that regard. That was just who I was. I really didn't want lose weight but in all reality I was tired of not being able to do a lot of things physically.

For a few days I was angry. I had made so much progress in my life: forgiving Dad and Mom, working on self-esteem. I thought I should be done with all the hard stuff. I didn't want to change. I shed a few tears. So many emotions and memories started floating into my mind from the past.

We checked into a couple different programs but decided they didn't line up with our lifestyle. We had tried so many things that we realized that the only thing that was truly going to help us this time was prayer. We already surrendered our whole lives to Jesus. Everything was given to the Lord over the past couple of years. Why not surrender this to the Lord as well?

It seems like a simple concept, but to Chris and I, it was profound. So we prayed and gave our food management issues to the Lord and asked for his discipline and strength to help us. Then we came up with a healthy eating game plan that worked for us and we started going to the gym. We drew our strength from the word of God:

For the spirit God gave us does not make us timid, but gives us power, love and self-discipline. (2 Timothy 1:7)

Inside my head, I continued to have a constant barrage of negative thoughts. Every bite of food I took inside my head I heard the word, "Fatass."

In my head I knew I was loved. I cherished what I read in the Bible about God's love. I constantly went back to a number of passages that were comforting to me. Yet, in my head, somehow I was always thinking that I was inadequate, unloved, and unworthy. My knowledge of God's love wasn't matching up with my inner thoughts.

I finally decided I was done!

I wanted it all gone!

I had shared a lot of my story with my dear friend Sarah. As a pastor's wife she is a wonderful listener and counselor. She wasn't surprised or overwhelmed by any of my past. I just wanted help to eat healthy and exercise, not dig up the past and other issues that were buried in relation to my weight, but deep down I knew it was time to deal with all of it. I was an emotional mess and was overwhelmed with memories and emotions. In fact, she brought new solutions that I hadn't ever known about. She suggested that we get together and pray in a way to deal with my demons. I wanted to be free of all I had dealt with for so many years. They had wreaked havoc over my life for far too long. It was time for a serious intervention.

I met with Sarah and some friends at her house and prayed one afternoon. I had two choices that day: step out in growth or step back into safety. I took everything they had to offer and we had a major breakthrough. I went home that afternoon fearless with a whole new outlook on life.

The following morning woke up and realized that my mind was quiet. There weren't any of the voices in my head. I didn't even know it was possible to feel like this!

I opened my Bible and read from the book of Psalms. I've always been comforted by the worship in the Psalms, but this time, I was struck with something new.

When the LORD restored the fortunes of Zion,
    we were like those who dreamed.
Our mouths were filled with laughter,
    our tongues with songs of joy.
Then it was said among the nations,
    "The Lord has done great things for them." (Psalm 126:1-2)

That verse captured how I felt! I was like one of the Israelites who longed to come back to their home. The demons were gone! Nothing was keeping me from Jesus. I had come home!

I read on in a few other areas of scripture and found joy everywhere I looked.

> He will yet fill your mouth with laughter
> and your lips with shouts of joy. (Job 8:21)

Together, Chris and I made strides towards better health. I no longer felt that I was being punished for having to take care of myself. My thoughts were geared towards "I need to get healthy" instead of "I have to eat healthy." I had another chance at taking better care of Chris. I was reminded that my body is the temple of the Holy Spirit and I need to treat it as such.

My personal self talk also changed. I stopped calling myself, "Fatass" at the gym. It wasn't something I drummed up within me, the words simply stopped. I stopped saying, "I can't." I have replaced that with saying, "I can."

> I can do all things through Him who gives me
> strength. (Philippians 4: 13)

I've drawn a lot of strength from Paul's words to the church in Philippi. The overarching concept "I can do all things" includes managing my weight.

My husband always reminds me, "You are stronger than you think you are."

I don't look in the mirror anymore and hear tapes playing in my mind. I no longer see what has been broken but rather what the Lord has restored. I cleaned out all my candy stashes as well as the pantry and the fridge. I even sent pictures to my friends of all the junk that I had thrown away. It was a simple but very liberating act.

There is a scale at the gym we go to – I don't keep one at home. When I step on the scale, I read the numbers and make a quick mental note. The numbers are secondary. I do not focus much on the scale anymore. My value is not placed in a number. I've learned to measure myself in strength, not pounds.

This chapter in my life has no ending as I will live and learn till the day that I die. I will continue to rejoice in the victories, both large and small. I will learn from the trials, speed bumps and other challenges that life throws my direction. I have been blessed with a support group of friends that have chosen to take a front seat in my life. They are faithful to be there through the tears of pain and tears of joy. They are my tribe.

God places people in our lives for a reason. Some become lifelong friends and some only help us through a season. Others are there for us to be a resource for them. Our friends and mentors are a blessing from the Lord. I hold them close and cherish them.

The more I heal from my past, the more I realize how much the Lord really was there even in times that I didn't think he was. He is my refuge, my healer, my daddy, and has been my protector my whole life. God doesn't intend for us to go through hurtful things; that is a result of man's sinful nature. Our choice is how we choose to deal with what has been hurt and broken.

In order to change, you have to love yourself. In order to love yourself, you need to know how much God loves you and care for you. A healthy view of God leads to a healthy view of yourself.

I have lived in both extremes – anorexic and obese. Dealing with my food issues is another level of healing that involves loving myself for who I am, the way I am, right where I am. I've found that loving yourself also comes in stages as we heal. It's a process that takes time, self-reflection, humility, and a deeper understanding of who I am in God's eyes. I have always been my own worst enemy and am well versed in self-destructive behavior. I'm an expert at punishing myself when I fail. Sometimes we need to let ourselves off the hook.

Our choice is how we decide to handle what life has handed us. God makes beautiful that which has been broken.

. . . . .

On the inside of my left arm just past the elbow, is a unique tattoo of a flowered skull. The forehead is a sunflower, the eye sockets are black with petals all around, the nose is heart shaped, and the jaws are colorful flowers. Surrounding the image are the words "Dry bones are Beautiful." It's not uncommon for people to ask me what my beautiful sugar skull tattoo means.

In the book of Ezekiel, Chapter 37, the prophet said, "The hand of the Lord was upon me, and he brought me out in the Spirit of the Lord and set me down in the middle of the valley; it was full of bones."

This isn't a scripture that is discussed in churches very often. It's quite graphic and describes the bones in a valley. "He led me around among them, and behold, there were very many on the surface of the valley, and behold, they were very dry."

God asked Ezekiel, "Can these dry bones live?"

As Ezekiel was standing among the army of dry bones he replied, "Oh Lord only you know."

That's pretty astute. Most of us would have simply looked at the death all around us and said, "Nope."

God said to Ezekiel, "Prophesy over these bones, and say to them, O dry bones, hear the word of the Lord. Thus says the Lord God to these bones: Behold, I will cause breath to enter you, and you shall live. And I will lay sinews upon you, and will cause flesh to come upon you, and cover you with skin, and put breath in you, and you shall live, and you shall know that I am the Lord."

Then an amazing thing happened, the story continues and Ezekiel said, "As I prophesied, there was a sound, and behold, a rattling sound, and the bones came together, bone to its bone. And I looked and behold, there were sinews on them, and flesh had come upon them, and skin had covered them. But there was no breath in them."

At this point Ezekiel must have been really freaked out. Imagine it! This would be worse than The Walking Dead! The valley was full of Zombies!

The story goes on, "Then he said to me, 'Prophesy to the breath ... Come from the four winds, O breath and breathe on these slain that they may live.' So I prophesied as he commanded me, and the breath came into them, and they lived and stood on their feet, an exceedingly great army."

Here's the conclusion God gave to Ezekiel, "These bones are the whole house of Israel. Behold, they say, 'Our bones are dried up and our hope is lost; we are indeed cut off.' Therefore prophesy, and say to them ... I will raise you from your graves and bring you into the land of Israel. And you shall know that I am the Lord."

The Lord instructed Ezekiel to command the dry bones to live again and they do. The breath is breathed into them again.

The reason I have dry bones tattooed on my skin is to be a reminder of my own dry dead past. Your past may be ugly, dry, broken, dead and hopeless, but through the Lord it can be brought back to life and restored into something beautiful. Just give it to Him. Dry bones can live again!

Chapter 23

"Keep your face to the sunshine and you cannot see the shadows.
It's what the sunflowers do."

Helen Keller

As you can tell from my story, I've been through a lot. If you've read this far, I don't need to tell you that my story is a difficult one. God made me with an inner strength that has allowed me to endure hardship and keep going.

I wonder what it was like when my wonderful triune God thought about making me. I imagine God sitting together at a kitchen table with Jesus and the Holy Spirit talking about my life plan and preparing to knit me together in my mother's womb. Stacks of files and paperwork cover the table, each file denoting all kinds of personality traits and varying degrees of physical parts that are available to use. As they make members of the human race. The three members of the trinity pulled out my file and started talking about me.

Jesus held a yellow legal pad in his hands. In his lap was a white three-ring binder with my name and number on the spine. He looked over the reports that will be made about my young life and says, "Father are you really going to allow her to be a part of all of that?"

God nodded and looked at his son. "I'm not doing those things to her. I wish she didn't have to go through any of that. I wish there was no sin. I don't want her mother to choose the life she chose. I don't want her father to be the man he was. But that's where she is going to be born. If Ramie is going to be there, then we will make her strong enough to endure every bit of it. And when she comes out on the other side of her childhood, she'll understand some of what we are up to."

The Holy Spirit had a painful look on his face, "I'll be working overtime with her."

Jesus looked at God and said, "I know what it means to undergo hardship. I'll be right there with her through everything. She won't know it at the time, but I'll be there."

God leaned back in his chair and put his hands behind his head. "When I sent you on your mission..." He stopped. His lower lip quivering, he couldn't form words for a moment, overwhelmed with the thought of his own son going to earth. "When I sent you, I knew that you would go through tremendous pain. You would teach, love, heal, and most importantly, forgive."

Jesus nodded. "I can't wait to see how she works out the forgiveness of her own parents, and how that draws her back to us."

God said, "Forgiveness is the basis of all relationships. We could talk about that all day long. Let's get back to Ramie. I don't want Ramie to have pain. I want her to have comfort."

The Holy Spirit interjected, "I'm all about that! You sent me to comfort the early church, and I've stayed ever since."

God continued, "But she is living in a fallen world and will be in a terrible situation from birth."

Jesus said, "Let's build her so that she'll be able to withstand everything she is exposed to."

God said, "Agreed. Let's get started."

Jesus opened a file on physical attributes, "She'll need an abnormally strong liver. It will have to degrade LSD before she is born. Then later on, it will have to purge alcohol from her bloodstream."

The Holy Spirit said, "She will have to withstand neglect."

Jesus picked up another file, "She will go through abuse that no kid should ever have to endure."

The Holy Spirit was weeping, "Let's make her bones strong enough and body durable enough to heal untreated broken bones. We'll make her esophagus and stomach strong enough to swallow drain cleaner and live to tell about it."

188

God gathered a few papers together. "I've got a few ideas for her back as well."

Jesus held three birth certificates in his hands. The names were listed for each of them: Micah, Rodney, and Tyler. He said, "If those babies are gonna be that big, we've got some serious problems."

God nodded, looking over the paperwork. He picked up a file and withdrew three papers from it.

Jesus saw what he was doing. He grabbed one of the papers out of God's hand and scanned it. Then he said, "Hey! Those body parts are usually reserved for Olympic athletes and war heroes."

The Holy Spirit beamed with delight, "Physical toughness, mental toughness and an inner strength. That's perfect."

Jesus turned his attention back to the three-ring binder and the birth certificates. "It will get her through, but won't last her whole life."

Holy Spirit said, "I'll be there when it finally fails."

God dug in and pulled out another paper. Jesus saw it and said, "A high pain threshold. She'll need that."

Jesus pulled out a picture of a sunflower. "This flower symbolizes worship and faithfulness."

God's eyes grew wide. He smiled, "It's good."

The Holy Spirit said, "Those flowers typically bloom in the summer. They are strong, with a firm foundation, and the roots go deep. They are tolerant of intense heat and droughts. They are resilient."

God said, "Like Ramie."

Jesus added, "The color is pure sunshine. The flower itself is pretty, feminine, and stocky. The center has many seeds. Each seed is a life that will be changed along the way because of her testimony. Each petal is it's own chapter."

The Holy Spirit said, "Put it all together and you have a strong, grounded, beautiful woman with a story to tell."

God said, "You know what I like best about sunflowers?"

Jesus and The Holy Spirit nodded, "Absolutely."

God continued, "All day long, the flower faces the sun. In the morning it faces east then tracks the yellow sun all day long until it sets in the west. I love it."

A tear fell from Jesus' face, "When people look to me, I'm right there with them. I hear every prayer. I'm the SON! I want people to look to me all day long."

The Holy Spirit said, "Let's put a passion for sunflowers in her heart."

God said, "I just love that girl so much."

Jesus said, "She's our girl."

God agreed, "Sure. A passion for sunflowers is appropriate for her."

Jesus laughed, "If we do that, she'll end up with them tattooed all over her body!"

The Holy Spirit said, "She'll put a tattoo at the base of her neck as a reminder to keep her head held up high. She will memorize Psalm 3:3 where David says 'God is my strength and he is the lifter of my head.' That's perfect."

Jesus added, "I expect her to have other sunflowers on her wrists to cover places where her dad broke her bones."

God added, "Every time she sees them, she'll remember us instead of her earthly father."

Jesus said, "She'll add imagery of adoption into the middle of a sunflower. She'll get deep with the symbolism."

The Holy Spirit said, "That will help bring healing after all she's been through. It will help her draw closer to us."

God said, "That settles it." He organized the papers and made a new a file with the name Ramie on the front. He waved his hand and under the name appeared a picture of a sunflower in full bloom.

Jesus said, "Beautiful."

The Holy Spirit said, "I love her already."

God said, "She's good."

Chapter 24

As I've shared my testimony with people over the years, some folks have told me that my story is full of some of the most horrific personal episodes that they have ever heard. I didn't choose my past. I didn't ask to be a victim of any of the things I have endured.

I didn't ask for my mother to be the person she was. I didn't ask for my father to treat me the way he did. I didn't ask for any of the things that I was put through. Seriously, who would do that? If you were about to be born on this planet and you could direct God to the family you wanted to go to, nobody would say, "Hey God, send me to that drug addicted prostitute." That just wouldn't happen. Most people would ask for a loving family with safety and freedom from harm.

I was born where I was born and I was raised where I was raised. But, if you haven't noticed, I'm not there anymore. I grew up. I'm a full-grown woman, with a full-grown husband. We have three kids and I'm looking forward to bouncing my grandkids on my knees and humming to them.

I *was* a victim.

The emphasis there is on the word *was*. I am no longer a victim. What I was is not what or who I am. As I look back on my past, every episode of my story has memories that are painful, yet Jesus Himself was there with me the whole time.

I didn't ask for the problems, but I also didn't ask Jesus to be with me through them. Yet He was. Every memory is flooded with

Jesus. He is my refuge, my healer, my Daddy, and has been my protector through every minute of my life.

We live in a world that God intended to be good. During the process of making the world, four times He said that it was good. Then when it was all done, God saw that it was very good (Genesis 1:31).

When sin entered the world, everything changed. Man's sinful nature completely altered God's very good creation. Our choice is how we choose to deal with what has been hurt and broken. When people ask, "Why did this happen to me?" They really aren't asking the proper question. The world is broken. Things are not as they should be. For as long as we live on this broken planet, we should always expect to have trouble.

The question we should ask is, *Why should we have anything good?* And as odd as it sounds, that's a great question, with a tremendous answer.

The answer is Jesus! The God of the universe did the most amazing things possible when He left His throne in heaven and came to live on the earth. He endured a life of hardship. The gospels Matthew, Mark, Luke and John tell Jesus' story. These four documents give four separate eyewitness accounts of Jesus' life. As we learn about his story, we can see a lot about this man that I've grown to love. I'm not going to go through every verse in the gospels, but let me point out a few details that might stick out.

My mother was a prostitute.

Jesus' his friends mocked Him through his childhood telling Him that His mother was a prostitute.

I was beaten and abused.

Jesus was beaten to the point of death.

Jesus knows my pain because He endured it while He lived here. Yet, God makes beautiful what has been hopeless, hurt, and broken!

The parallels go on and on. Everything I have gone through was equaled in Jesus' life. He never sinned, yet He endured every kind of pain and trouble.

God doesn't intend for us to go through hurtful things. All of that is a result of man's sinful nature.

192

. . . . .

One beautiful sunny morning, I was home alone. My house was in shambles and desperately needed to be cleaned, but I was tired and frustrated. I managed to put away the dishes and clean my kitchen floor but I couldn't bring myself to look at the laundry or even think about any of the other things I needed to get done. I sat down and worked my way through the next chapter in a Beth Moore Bible study. I read about a boy going down to a river to retrieve water. His broken pot was leaking the precious water drop by drop all the way back to his house. Eventually he was very frustrated until an older man said to him, "Look at your side of the road. The flowers on the road have been watered, tremendous beauty has came from your cracked pot."

Suddenly I realized – *I'm a cracked pot.*

I went to the garage and found a ceramic flowerpot that I had and walked back to the kitchen. I held it in my hands and felt the light brown pot's roughened surface. It had order. It was made a certain way with a thickened rim to strengthen the top, and sturdy sides all around it.

I leaned against my kitchen counter and thought about how my life had been broken. Against my will, my life was in pieces. It was as if the separate sections of my life were strewn all over the place. I looked back at the pot. It had precision and was clean and orderly. My life was not like this pot.

In a moment of irrational reverse creativity, I went back to the garage and grabbed a hammer. I returned to the pot and stood over it for a minute. If that pot was symbolic, it would have to be in pieces. With the hammer in my hand, I gave it a violent blow. As the metal made contact with the porcelain, it shattered into a dozen pieces that were strewn all across the table. I recognized this pattern. The chaos was familiar. As I sat down at the kitchen table, I saw my life.

Broken.

Shattered.

In some distorted way, this was comforting to me. I finally had a picture of what I had been through. The pieces of the pot were big and small. Some were sitting all by themselves, lonely. Other pieces were piled on top of one another or leaning against a wall. That chaos was my life.

I didn't pick up the pieces, or start to sweep up the dust. I had no intention of cleaning up this mess. This mess was MY mess. I would leave it for as long as I chose to leave it. The potsherds lay on the table like wounded soldiers after a battle.

Then something occurred to me.

I reached down and picked up one of the larger pieces and held it in my hands. I felt the sharp edge with my finger. This piece could cut me if I wasn't careful. It was dangerous. I looked back at the floor, every one of the pieces was sharp, threatening, potentially debilitating. The piece in my hand didn't seem to have a home. It was all by itself. But I saw it as a part of me, a part of my story.

I opened up a drawer and fumbled around in it for a minute. My junk drawer was full of things that needed to be organized and cleaned. I saw pens, a candle, and then what I was looking for, a Sharpie. I leaned over the kitchen counter and wrote the word "Abuse" on the broken piece. I held the broken piece in my hands and realized that it was a piece of my story. I was broken, and abused. My eyes welled up as I was once again flooded with memories of being threatened at gunpoint, tied up, beaten, …

The ceramic piece had drops of my tears on it several minutes later. I looked over and realized that the drawer was still open and my eyes fell on a small bottle of industrial strength glue.

I had glue!

I picked up another piece about the same size as the first one. I wrote the word "Fear" on it. Again, the emotional connection with the piece of my life that was symbolized by the broken piece of pottery was intense. Fortunately, I was alone for an extended period of time and nobody was going to be in my kitchen for a while. I held both pieces in my hands and the two of them fit together. I picked up the glue and ran a bead along the edge and secured the two pieces together.

I took my time. One by one, I reached down and picked up the pieces of my life and set them on the kitchen table. I named and labeled them: perfectionism, anger, divorce, rejection, hopeless, …

Then, through a process laden with the emotions that accompany the labels, Jesus and I sat at the table and looked at the project. Together, we pieced the broken pieces together one at a time. As I ran the glue along the edges and pressed the pieces together I saw the glue seep through the cracks. My pot was crying just as I was.

In my mind's eye, I had hoped that the pieces would go back together perfectly without any defect or change but that wasn't happening. I was starting to get discouraged. My pot was not turning out perfect. I continued to fix the shattered stoneware vessel one segment at a time. Finally, all the major pieces were together and I set my life down on the table to dry. I waited for the glue to dry and saw the dust and remnants that still remained on the table. It was still a mess. The glue lines finally dried as scars along the crack lines where it had been mended.

I sat with Jesus for a while longer and it became clear to me that over the past few years, He had taken the broken pieces of my life and mended them back together. He didn't do this all at once. I wouldn't have been able to process everything in a single day. For me, it would have been too much both emotionally and physically. But each of the pieces, one at a time, as I've surrendered them to Him, He has taken, brushed off, applied the glue, and pressed back together.

The scars are still there. They will always be there. They are from a battle well fought and won. Every one of my scars is a symbol for me – a sign of victory. My pot had been through a journey. It was broken and scattered all over my floor. Then it was pieced together but there were still some holes that would not be filled. I suppose that these holes are areas where the edges had morselized upon impact and became a myriad of tiny pieces that couldn't be rectified. I cleaned the table before my husband came home but the resultant holes could never be filled.

The process of putting my life back together had been enlightening and rejuvenating for me but I didn't want a life with holes. I wanted the pot to be used for flowers. What good is a pot with holes in it?

I was once again frustrated. The original purpose of the pot was gone. If I plant a flower in it, the dirt would pour out of the sides, it couldn't be used for a sunflower. What can it be used for now?

I looked back at the open drawer and saw the mess within it. *I should really clean up that drawer.* I picked up the candle and started sorting through the drawer to see what else I could take out of the drawer to organize better. There was a lighter, some pens and other junk. I looked back at the pot. Suddenly, a thought hit me.

With the candle and lighter in hand, I closed the drawer and walked back over to my precious broken pot. With the care of an artist as she looks at her new creation, I placed the candle inside the pot. I flicked the lighter and allowed the flame to meet the candle's wax-encrusted wick. As the candle came to life, the little fire burned brightly within the cracked pot. Light shone through cracks to the outside world.

The words rang out from each and every piece. I had written perfectionism, anger, divorce, rejection, hopeless, and many others. These words speak of pain, trial, and tribulation. They are personal to me. They are my words. They represent my memories, my story.

The pot was me, my testimony.

I sat down at my table with the pot. It was no longer a flowerpot and would never hold a flower. But I was pleased with its new purpose. It had been transformed into a lamp and the light shines inside it as the light of Jesus shines through the scars and imperfections of my life. Jesus helped me see every piece of the pot as a victory. Every scar line that holds the pieces together is a victory. Every crack and hole that allows the light to come out is a victory.

I am a victory.

But as I sat at the table watching the light beam through the cracks in the earthenware pot, I realized that these words are not alone. Each of these words has an antonym, a descriptor of the opposite of the pain, trial, and tribulation. For every word like anger, there is another word like joy. For divorce, there is commitment. For rejection, there is acceptance. Perfectionism is countered with grace. Jesus provided the opposites. The antonyms. Each of the words that I wrote with the Sharpie is countered with a better word from Jesus.

The pot is not who I am today. It may be who I was, but it is not who I AM. Neither is it who I will become. Where I'm going is not where I've been.

I am no longer a victim.

I have obtained victory.

I have victory in Jesus.

This is my story. I'm sure it's different from yours, but we all can learn from one another.

Have you ever thought of your life like a pot?
What does your pot look like?
Who is shining through the cracks?
My prayer is that Jesus shines in your life as He has in mine.

If you would like to contact me,
you can find me on Facebook

Ramie Smith Stenzel

www.ingramcontent.com/pod-product-compliance
Lightning Source LLC
LaVergne TN
LVHW011228080426
835509LV00005B/389